# THE CUSTOMER
# IS KEY

# THE CUSTOMER IS KEY

## Gaining An Unbeatable Advantage Through Customer Satisfaction

**MILIND M. LELE**

SLC Consultants
Chicago, Illinois

**WITH JAGDISH N. SHETH**

University of Southern California
Los Angeles, California

John Wiley & Sons
New York / Chichester / Brisbane / Toronto / Singapore

*To Babumama,*
*and to Evangeline*

**Library of Congress Cataloging-in-Publication Data**

Lele, Milind M.
  The customer is key.

  (Wiley management series on problem solving,
  decision making, and strategic thinking)
  Bibliography: p.
  1. Consumer satisfaction.  I. Title.  II. Series.
HF5415.3.L45   1987       658.8'12      87-21549
ISBN 0-471-82859-9

Printed in the United States of America

10  9  8  7  6  5

# Preface

This book is for everyone who cares about the customer; it's not just for people in marketing and sales, but for the business community as a whole. The message is simple: "Customer satisfaction is key to long-term profitability and keeping the customer happy is *everybody's* business." Increasingly, companies are finding that factors such as lower labor costs, more efficient manufacturing, and superior technology provide only transient, short-term advantages. In the long run, however, what matters is how pleased the customer is with a company's products. If customers are happy with the value delivered by the firm's products, if they feel they are valued and treated fairly, they will stay loyal to the firm for a long time. Otherwise, they'll switch at the first opportunity.

I began this book over 10 years ago, when I was asked by a client, a large machinery manufacturer, to analyze how after-sales support affected customer satisfaction. Initially I concentrated solely on the operational and logistical aspects, that is, improved parts availability, more training for service technicians, built-in diagnostics, loaners for extended failures, and so forth. However, I was surprised to find that, despite significant improvements in these areas, customers were still unhappy.

Upon analyzing the problem in more detail, I came to realize that nobody really knew what the customer wanted and needed by way of after-sales support. As a result, management was getting a fragmented picture, one that depended to a large extent on which department was doing the talking. In this milieu, customers wanted better parts availability (the parts department), higher reliability (engineering), more training for the service technicians (service), or easier-to-read manuals (technical publications). The net result was that every year the firm was spending more money on after-sales support and getting less in return for its efforts.

This initial assignment led to further research on customer expectations regarding after-sales support. Out of this research evolved techniques for developing comprehensive support strategies that avoided the sub-optimization described previously.[1]

Up to this point I had concentrated my attention on industrial and business machinery, for example, tractors, combines, computers, copiers, and so on. My next step was to look at customer satisfaction more broadly. I wanted to find out how satisfied customers were, overall, what made them dissatisfied, and why companies failed to keep them happy.

I was most interested to discover many of the same symptoms and problems that I had first encountered when studying service and support problems in industrial equipment. Once again, I was amazed to find that very few firms seemed to know what would keep their customers satisfied and happy. Consequently there was the same fragmentation and sub-optimization that I had observed earlier in industrial equipment. Further, there was the pervasive sense that "customer satisfaction is marketing's, or (as was more often the case) the complaint's department's problem."

I gradually came to realize that the root cause was the same: Companies and their managers appear to have forgotten that *profit comes from keeping the customer happy*. Despite the vast expenditures on market research, advertising, promotion and other "mar-

---

[1]These researches have been described in "Good Product Support is Smart Marketing," by Milind M. Lele and Uday S. Karmarkar, *Harvard Business Review*, Nov.-Dec., 1983, and in "How Service Needs Influence Product Design," by Milind M. Lele, *Sloan Management Review*, Fall 1985.

keting" efforts, we appear to have lost sight of the fundamental fact that (as one of the people interviewed for this book put it), " . . . if the customer is not satisfied, he (or she) is not going to be a customer tomorrow, and if he is not a customer tomorrow, we don't have a business tomorrow." In short, we're paying lip service to the marketing concept.

At this point I decided to find out (1) whether the marketing concept was still valid, and (2) if the answer was "Yes," which firms were really implementing this concept and how did they go about it. A number of factors made it difficult to establish a clear relationship between customer satisfaction and profitability in all industries. However, research conducted by the PIMS project at the Harvard Business School had shown that superior product "quality" led to higher profits. Further, when I analyzed the farm equipment and automotive industries, I found a clear relationship between customer satisfaction and profitability. In farm equipment, market shares of the individual firms were extremely closely related to customer satisfaction; the happier the customer, the higher the firm's share, and vice versa. In automobiles, there was a similar close relationship between customer's satisfaction and their willingness to buy the same make of car again. There was a similar, but much less pronounced pattern in the airline industry.

To answer the second question, I analyzed a number of industries and identified "winners"—companies that were leaders in *both* customer satisfaction and long-term financial performance. These firms represented a cross-section of managerial styles, growth patterns and internal cultures. I ended up studying 15 firms in 13 diverse industries, covering everything from aerospace to residential real estate services, overnight package delivery, and food service distribution. Inevitably, this was a limited sample. There were a number of other firms meeting the twin criteria of superior performance and customer satisfaction that I would have liked to study, but could not do so due to limitations of time and money.

At each of these companies I interviewed executives at all levels, analyzed internal systems, policies and procedures, and reviewed internal reports. Without exception the firms were extremely cooperative, and provided an in-depth look at their operations.

The results reinforced my previous conclusions: *These firms were successful precisely because they made customer satisfaction, at a profit, their top priority*. I don't mean to imply that they're perfect; far from it. Nearly all of them, at one time or another, have had problems with customers and/or with maintaining their profit levels. Some of these problems are well-known: Jaguar came back from the brink of insolvency in 1980, Deere is still struggling in a stagnant farm equipment market, and Xerox has yet to regain its supremacy in office equipment. But year in and year out, these firms have concentrated on customer satisfaction as *the* key to building a profitable business, and on the whole, they have succeeded handsomely.

This field research also helped identify the specific reasons these firms were able to achieve the dual goal of superior customer satisfaction and superior profitability. While I identified a number of factors that contributed significantly, one thing stood out: *These companies had a balanced approach*. Put another way, at every company I asked the question, "What's the key to your success?" and consistently the answer was, "There's no one secret, it's a whole host of things." These firms concentrated on making certain that every element that contributed to customer satisfaction—product design, manufacturing, sales messages, sales attitudes, channel selection, after-sales support, complaint handling, incentives, and symbols—was focussed on the same goal, namely, superior customer satisfaction, at a profit.

Competitiveness is currently a hot idea. Companies and managers are keenly interested in it, researchers are actively looking into it, and there's even talk of national programs on improving competitiveness. But I often think that we're in danger of overlooking the most important competitive weapon: happy customers. All said and done, a satisfied customer is a loyal customer, one who is willing to give a firm time to adapt to changes in labor costs, technologies and market needs.

# *Acknowledgements*

This book would not have been possible without the enthusiastic participation and support of many people on two continents. The companies discussed in this book were very helpful in providing access to key executives, supplying internal reports and studies and responding to follow-up questions. I would like to thank the coordinators at each of these companies for their flexibility in scheduling interviews, often at short notice, and their forbearance at some of my more intrusive questions! The executives interviewed were most forthcoming and discussed the various issues without reservation, describing their operations and approaches at length and in considerable detail. I am most grateful.

Especial thanks to the following: David Ely, Bernhard Oettli and Jim Peterson, all of whom went to great lengths to assist by letting me use their firms' extensive customer databases, surveys and other information. Dave Power, who very kindly provided unfettered access to his firm's extensive information bank on the automotive industry, which considerably enhanced the statistical basis of the argument. Buck Rodgers, who gave freely of his time to discuss how IBM kept the customer happy; he also reviewed the manuscript and provided needed encouragement. Phil Kotler, Harry Davis and Dave Wilson, who read early drafts of the manuscript and made valuable suggestions.

Two researchers were central to this two-year effort. Tracie Baker came in at the beginning and ensured that the research (and the writing) got into gear. In the second half of the project, Virginia Cram made a vital contribution by double-checking all my references, editing the entire manuscript once again and generally making sure that I met various publishing deadlines. Finally, at the very end Kathleen Bougère and Jenny Yocom did sterling work in proofreading. My thanks to them all; as they know full well, I couldn't have done it without them.

I owe a special debt of gratitude to David Ewing, who first suggested I write a book on this subject and persuaded John Wiley & Sons of the merits of the project. Subsequently, John Mahaney, my editor, maintained his faith in the concept of the book and patiently endured several delays and other vicissitudes. I would like to thank them both. Thanks also to the Wiley staff, particularly Tom Gilmartin, John Ponder, and Kathleen Kelly, for their tolerance and support.

Last but not least, my interest in business and commerce was stimulated by my uncle, Baburao Kelkar. He has always pointed out the crucial importance of the customer; therefore it is fitting that this book be dedicated to him.

# Contents

# 1

# *Happy Customers*

## *THE UNBEATABLE ADVANTAGE*

Keeping customers happy is the best defense against competition. The firm that keeps its customers happy is virtually unbeatable. Its customers are more loyal. They buy more, more often. They're willing to pay more for the firm's products, and they stick with the firm through difficult periods, allowing it time to adapt to change.

### *Nothing Else Comes Close*

Nothing matches the long-term protection that keeping customers happy provides.

☐ *New Inventions Don't.* "If you make a better mousetrap, the world will beat a path to your door." Yes, for about as long as it takes your neighbor to copy it, improve it, and offer it at half your price. IBM introduced the PC in late 1981 and the first "clones" were available in early 1983. Today, clones account for half of all PCs sold.

☐ *Technology Doesn't.* New processes, incremental changes to old processes, investments in automation—none of these holds off competition for long. Studies indicate that 60 to 90 percent of all learning leaks away to competitors within a very short period of time.

☐ *Lower Labor Costs Don't.* In the 1960s Detroit looked over its shoulder at the lower labor costs of the Europeans. In the 1970s, the Europeans scrambled to keep ahead of the Japanese. Today the Japanese are running scared of the South Koreans. Tomorrow, the South Koreans will be sprinting to keep ahead of the Chinese, Brazilians, and Indians. There is always someone willing to work for less.

☐ *Regulation Doesn't.* The Japanese computer industry is highly protected, yet IBM holds 45 percent of the market. "Voluntary" import curbs on their cars merely helped the Japanese to attack Detroit's profitable midsized car market. Governmental protection is a temporary and often ineffective barrier against competitors. If there is a market worth having, competitors will find a way around any and all regulation.

☐ *Size Doesn't.* In the early 1960s, General Motors held over 50 percent of the U.S. market. Today its share is under 40 percent and shrinking. Focusing on niches doesn't help either. Wal-Mart, the discount merchandiser, grew by focusing on Southern towns that were too small for the larger chains. Today, however, these small towns have become big cities; good-bye to Wal-Mart's competitive advantage.

All these techniques for holding off the competition offer at best only short-term relief.

### The Idea Is Not New

Keeping customers happy is the very basis of the marketing concept that many firms claim to follow. In a classic *Harvard Business Review* article written in 1960, Ted Levitt said, "(T)he view that an industry is a customer-satisfying process, not a goods-producing process, is vital for all businessmen to understand. An industry begins with the customer and his needs, not with a patent, a raw material, or a selling skill." Levitt went on, "A truly marketing-minded firm tries to create value-satisfying goods and services that consumers will want to buy." David Ogilvy, founder of Ogilvy & Mather, put it even more simply: "The consumer is your wife."

In that case this marriage is falling apart. In industry after industry customer dissatisfaction is growing. Customers are less loyal to traditional, long established brands and suppliers. They are more willing to try new sources.

☐ *Automobiles.* U.S. car buyers have deserted Detroit's products in favor of Japanese and European imports. In 1986, one out of every four cars sold in the U.S. market was imported.

☐ *Retailing.* Department stores and mass merchandisers such as Saks Fifth Avenue and Sears have lost much of their traditional clientele to off-price stores, specialty outlets, and catalogs.

☐ *Color TVs.* U.S. firms have lost many of their customers to Japanese and South Korean brands which today hold over 45 percent, a lion's share, of the U.S. market.

☐ *Raw Materials.* U.S. steel buyers have abandoned their long-standing loyalty to domestically produced steel in favor of overseas suppliers. Today imported steel accounts for over 20 percent of the total U.S. market.

While other factors such as lower labor rates, an over-valued dollar, and governmental subsidies also played a role, customer dissatisfaction was a major cause. Car buyers became disgruntled with Detroit's poor quality and indifference to customer complaints. U.S. TV producers alienated a powerful group of customers—the mass merchandisers such as Sears—when they refused to manufacture private label color TVs, opening the door for Japanese imports. Department stores alienated loyal shoppers with high prices and poor service, while steel buyers were offended by Big Steel's arrogance.

As these and other examples indicate, apparently companies have not been able to translate the marketing concept into practice. This is not for want of trying; in the 25 years since Levitt's article first appeared in print, companies have invested huge sums of money in marketing and in becoming customer-oriented. In the United States alone, marketing expenditures have increased from $2.6 billion in 1960 to over $300 billion in 1986. During this same time period the membership of the American Marketing Association has grown fivefold from 8,600 members in 1960 to 50,000 in 1986.

### What Happened?

Is the marketing concept a myth? If not, why have most firms failed to put it into practice? Have any firms succeeded in making the marketing concept work? What have they done that's different? Why did they do it? What factors are responsible for their success? Are they specific to a given industry or can they be applied elsewhere?

We decided to try and find the answers to these questions. First, we surveyed a number of industries from aircraft manufacturing to fast food to see if we could find any firms that had succeeded in both keeping customers happy *and* earning high profits. From this survey we identified a number of "winners" (as we came to call them). We then researched 15 of these winners, representing 10 very diverse industries, in depth through on-site interviews with some of their key executives, analyses of their internal reports, reviews of secondary sources, such as trade publications and general business magazines, and discussions with industry experts. Next we researched the "losers"—firms that had failed spectacularly at keeping customers happy—using secondary sources. We would have liked to have interviewed the managers of these firms, but this idea had to be abandoned for lack of willing participants!

We then familiarized ourselves with the consumer's viewpoint via publications, survey data, and research reports. In addition we interviewed two organizations containing considerable amounts of data regarding customer satisfaction: Consumers Union in Mt. Vernon, New York and the firm of J.D. Power and Associates in Westlake Village, California. Consumers Union provided us with a comprehensive overview of buyers' satisfaction levels with a number of different types of products such as electrical and electronic gadgets and appliances, consumer electronics such as TVs and VCRs, automobiles, and services. J.D. Power and Associates conducts an annual survey of car buyer satisfaction; we used these surveys in our analysis of customer satisfaction in the automotive industry.

Finally, we tried to quantify the exact relationship between customer satisfaction and profitability. As one might expect, this proved to be difficult; in many industries the necessary data simply weren't available. However, for the automotive and farm equipment industries we were able to gather enough information to study the customer satisfaction and profitability relationship closely.

## WHAT WE DISCOVERED

After two years of research, we're now in a position to answer the questions we asked earlier. Specifically, we have come to the following conclusions:

☐ The marketing concept works
☐ The key issue is cost versus customer
☐ Most companies are cost-focused
☐ The winners' secret is their holistic approach

### The Marketing Concept Works

Our winners are living, breathing proof that keeping customers happy is the best defense against competition. Each has made providing superior customer satisfaction a cornerstone of its entire approach to business. This strategy has paid off handsomely. These firms' products and services consistently command higher prices in the marketplace. Their customers are more loyal; 12 out of the 15 firms we researched have maintained or increased their market shares over the past decade. Further, their customers tend to stay with them; one company even came back spectacularly from the brink of failure because of its customers' affection for its products. The net result is that these firms have consistently been more profitable than their competitors while, at the same time, providing superior customer satisfaction.

### The Key Issue Is Cost versus Customer

How a company resolves this trade-off in every aspect of its business—product design, manufacturing, sales, after-sales support, and so on—determines whether it will be successful in implementing the marketing concept.

### Most Companies Are Cost-Focused

In general, keeping customers happy merely gets lip service; management attention is concentrated on cutting costs. This explains why the vast majority of firms have failed to put the marketing concept into practice despite large investments in marketing.

### The Winners' Secret Is Their Holistic Approach

The overwhelming difference between the winners and the rest lies not in *what* they do, but rather *how* they do it. There are few if any differences between these firms and their counterparts in terms of market research, the design and manufacturing of products, the sales techniques they use, or their after-sales support and service. The critical difference lies in the fact that, throughout the organization, there is an emphasis on *customer satisfaction at a profit*. These firms never forget either of these goals, and their success lies in their ability to take an integrated, holistic approach that balances these two often conflicting requirements without compromising either customers or the bottom line. In other words, unlike other firms, our winners don't suboptimize; they don't leave customer satisfaction to the salesforce while everyone else pursues departmental objectives: cutting costs, improving labor relations, finding cheaper raw materials, or whatever.

## THE BASIC CONFLICT: COST VERSUS CUSTOMER

"Cut costs? Or keep customers happy?" This dilemma is at the heart of the problem. In their search for a long-term competitive edge, managers are finding that superior technology, low-cost labor, or cheaper raw materials are, at best, of limited value. How then can a firm earn higher profits than its competitors? In a competitive marketplace, a firm has two fundamental choices:

1. *It Can Cut Costs.* Here the firm says, "Prices are set by the market and there's nothing we can do about it. Therefore, let's be

more efficient than all the others to ensure that we make more money." Maximizing profit, under this approach, means minimizing costs while making sure that customer satisfaction is at least equal to that provided by competing products.

2. *It Can Maximize Customer Satisfaction.* As an alternative to minimizing costs, the firm can say, "We will earn above-average profits by making the customer as happy as we can while keeping costs under control." The firm's goal is to maximize customer satisfaction and thereby obtain higher profitability through the ability to charge more for its products than its rivals, obtain more repeat business, and reduce its marketing and sales expenses.

### They're Not the Same

Cutting costs and maximizing customer satisfaction are not two sides of the same coin. The two goals demand different approaches to product design, to manufacturing, to sales—in short, to every aspect of the firm's operations. The first strategy says, "We will produce and market a parity product—one that performs as well as most competitors' offerings—more efficiently than any of our adversaries." The second strategy says, "Customers will pay more for a product that really makes them happy, so let's find out what that product is and how we can make it with reasonable efficiency."

To understand the difference between these two philosophies, consider how Texas Instruments (TI) and Hewlett-Packard (HP) attacked the market for hand-held calculators in the 1970s. From the outset, TI focused on being the low-cost producer. It cut prices aggressively, in advance of costs, and invested heavily in manufacturing facilities to take advantage of the latest innovations. TI's calculators were functional; they did the job at a very competitive price. However, the calculators didn't necessarily maximize customer satisfaction: the keyboard did not have the smoothest touch, some of the functions were awkward to perform, and the displays were difficult to read, especially if viewed from an angle.

By contrast, HP avoided the mass market and concentrated on customers it knew best: scientists, engineers, financial analysts, and MBAs. It wasn't the low-cost producer, nor did it try to become one. Instead, HP concentrated on designing machines that maximized customer satisfaction. This focus was evident in several features: The keys were more responsive to the touch, providing a reassuring "click" as tactile feedback; and the displays could be read at almost any angle. There were a number of different models, each tailored for an individual market. The manuals were well-written and clear, leading the reader step-by-step through all the features and capabilities of each of the machines. Everything about these calculators—the external styling, keyboard layouts, accompanying literature—was designed to let the customer know that this machine would be easy to use and would provide a high degree of satisfaction. HP's calculators were far from cheap; they often cost substantially more than competing TI models. What HP promised—and provided, as their success demonstrates—was greater satisfaction for the buyer.

### Key Differences

Fundamentally, cost minimization takes an internal, production-centered view. It treats the customers' needs as a given and makes the organization's goal that of meeting these needs as efficiently as possible. The alternative, customer-oriented, approach is externally focused. It challenges the firm to find ways of making and keeping customers as satisfied as possible, subject to the requirement that the firm be profitable. These divergent views lead to important differences between the two strategies:

☐ Firms that concentrate on maximizing customer satisfaction tend to be more willing to make long-term investments in projects whose impact can be felt only after several years, such as customer hotlines, extended warranty programs, and additional product features to improve customer convenience.

☐ These customer-oriented firms are also more prepared to take a short-term "hit" in profits if they believe it is necessary to achieve their overall goal of keeping the customer happy. For example: They will accept lower profit levels on a particular product rather than eliminate features or benefits that the customer associates with their offerings.

☐ Firms that concentrate on minimizing costs tend to be functional in their orientation, especially where the customer is concerned. Knowing the customer's needs and wants is considered the marketing department's responsibility; the other functions stick to their own knitting. Customer-focused organizations, by contrast, make it everyone's business to know the customer intimately. In such companies, designers, engineers, manufacturing personnel, assembly workers, support staff, and senior executives all participate in meetings with customers and take pride in knowing about customers' wants, complaints, and problems.

### Soft Opinions versus Hard Facts

These differences are not accidental or superficial. Rather, they are the direct result of the different philosophies embodied in the two approaches.

Cost minimization assumes that the company knows what the customer wants, can specify the degree of satisfaction required for a parity product in the marketplace, and can make the changes needed to create this product. Provided that we can measure customer satisfaction precisely, this approach will indeed work.

Unfortunately, it is very difficult to measure something as intangible as how happy buyers are with a particular product or service. Consequently, the cost-minimization approach inevitably loads the dice in favor of investments and actions whose impact can be measured and translated into dollars and cents. In any discussion of how to allocate resources, the costs of investments to improve customer satisfaction are known virtually down to the last penny, while the benefits are often difficult to evaluate. With cost minimization, marketing is always fighting a losing battle. It is continually forced to defend its opinions or qualitative assessments against the precise numbers prepared by accounting, engineering, or manufacturing departments—soft opinions versus hard facts. Inevitably, the company becomes biased toward cost-cutting and moves away from long-term investments in customer satisfaction whose impact is inherently difficult to quantify.

The E-coat painting process at Ford provides a vivid example of the difficulties this cost-focus creates for proponents of investments in improving customer satisfaction. In 1958 Ford invented this process to improve the quality of the paint jobs, particularly the rustproofing of the underbodies of cars and trucks. The process was a success from the start, and soon became an industry standard. However, it proved exceptionally difficult to get the process adopted within Ford itself. The reason? Cost.

> (I)t would cost about $4 million or $5 million a plant. Since there were 20 plants, the total figure was large, just under $100 million. The men who had developed E-coat and the plant men who pushed for it considered it the key to a great increase in quality. Unfortunately, there was no way to quantify that improvement in terms of sales. That it was a much better process no one doubted. But when the manufacturing and product men pointed to its virtues, the finance men pointed to the price. Somehow the manufacturing men would be unable to *prove* [emphasis in original] that E-coat would make a $4 million difference. . . . Runyon [a senior Ford manufacturing executive] would keep saying that it [E-coat] was incomparably better, and the finance men would say, oh it was better, no doubt of that, finance would take his word for that, but was it really *that* much better, was it worth all those millions, could he *prove* the benefits? No, of course he could not. At those

meetings he always ended up, like others before him, on the defensive; he would go in confident of what he intended to say, and when it was over he had somehow failed. (David Halberstam, *The Reckoning*, William Morrow, New York, 1986)

## When Is Maximizing Customer Satisfaction Not Important?

Under certain conditions, the cost-minimization strategy makes economic sense, and the alternative approach of maximizing customer satisfaction may be impractical, uneconomic, or even downright ruinous. We can group these situations into the following categories:

☐ *When the Buyer Has No Recourse.* In some cases the dissatisfied buyer has no economic, legal, or moral recourse. This occurs, for example, in sales that are "as is, where is" with no possibility of repeat transactions, such as certain residential real estate transactions. It can also occur when the supplier has a lot of power, for example, monopolies or cartels. The diamond cartel, for instance, is said to be indifferent to the level of satisfaction of its immediate customer, the diamond dealer.

☐ *When the Buyer Has An Extremely Short Memory.* A basic premise of maximizing customer satisfaction is that the happy buyer will remember the supplier and remain loyal in future purchases. In some situations, the buyer's memory is poor or nonexistent. Then it doesn't pay to maximize customer satisfaction. Many government purchases are, by law, "memory-less"; contracts must be awarded to the lowest bidder, regardless of the level of satisfaction the vendor previously provided.

☐ *When the Buyer Cannot or Will Not Pay a Price Premium for Higher Levels of Satisfaction.* Under these circumstances, it would be uneconomic to add costs to the product that cannot be recovered through a higher price. Government procurements fall into this category, as do the price-sensitive segments of any market.

☐ *When the Customer Faces Penalties for Expressing Dissatisfaction.* In a dictatorship, it may be worth as much as a customer's life to express dissatisfaction with the product. At other times, the disincentives may be economic and nearly as effective: You're a collector who recently acquired two paintings by a renowned artist for $50,000. Upon examination, you realize they're rather shoddy works done by his pupils. The artist refuses to admit this or to discuss the matter further. Do you make your dissatisfaction public and see the value of your investment plummet? Or do you quietly get rid of the paintings?

☐ *When Other Purchasers Ignore the Dissatisfied Customer.* In some cases, other buyers may disregard the negative views of a dissatisfied customer, such as the unhappy purchaser of a lottery ticket who fails to win the prize.

☐ *When the Incremental Costs Outweigh the Additional Profit.* Occasionally, the incremental costs of maximizing customer satisfaction will be considerably higher than the price premium that most customers will pay. For example, this is the case when made-to-measure clothing is compared to standard sizes.

### *When Does It Make Sense To Maximize Customer Satisfaction?*

If the buyer has recourse when he or she is unhappy, or if providing superior customer satisfaction creates a cost to the customer for changing suppliers (a switching cost); then it is economic for the firm to try to maximize customer satisfaction.

☐ *When the Buyer Has Legal Recourse.* Buyers in many transactions have contractual or statutory rights in case they're dissatisfied. Consumer protection laws, for example, regulate warranties, misrepresentation, disclosure of financing terms, and so on. It may be preferable to minimize litigation costs by maximizing customer satisfaction.

☐ *When the Buyer Has Verbal Recourse.* In some markets purchasers' comments can make or break a firm. This is particularly true in small, closed markets, such as the diamond exchanges in New York and Antwerp, the London stock exchange prior to deregulation, and the Marwari community of financiers in India. In these places a dissatisfied buyer's vocal complaints can easily lead to strong, immediate reprisals. The offending firm finds that no one will do business in the future with it; the market has silently voted to exclude the firm.

☐ *When the Buyer Has Economic Recourse.* Legal and verbal recourse are not nearly as strong a weapon as economic recourse. Customers have economic recourse when sales create a continuing relationship or the possibility of one. Such ongoing relationships can be created through the need for continuing after-sales support, the purchase of peripheral equipment and supplies, and the mutual expectation that future purchases are contingent on the level of satisfaction with the current transaction. Such relationships are commonly found in industrial purchases of raw materials, supplies, and capital equipment.

## *CAN THEY CO-EXIST?*

Can a firm simultaneously maximize customer satisfaction and minimize costs? In other words, can managers have their cake and eat it too?

In theory, it can't happen. No company can keep all of its customers as happy as possible while cutting costs to the lowest level in order to become a cost leader. The reason is the nature of the relationship between customer satisfaction and product or service costs. As customer satisfaction increases, so do costs. This is the law of diminishing returns. It costs the firm far more to go from 90 to 95 percent customer satisfaction than to increase satisfaction from 85 to 90 percent. (Figure 1.1a) Therefore, we cannot simply say, "maximize customer satisfaction"; without some explicit or implicit constraints on costs, the statement doesn't make sense. Similarly, "become a cost leader" or "minimize cost" is meaningful only when we add the requirement of meeting a specified, minimum level of customer satisfaction. We cannot have both. We cannot maximize customer satisfaction *and* minimize costs. (Figure 1.1b)

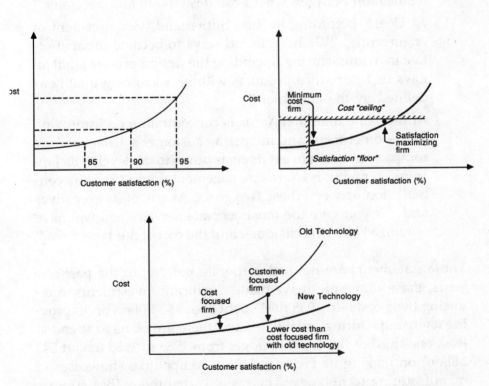

*Figure 1.1(a) Marginal costs increase with customer satisfaction, (b) Minimize cost or maximize satisfaction, (c) How new technology affects cost position*

Under competitive pressures, however, some of the winners we studied are trying to do just that—to keep maximizing customer satisfaction while getting costs down to the levels of their most efficient competitors.

☐ According to Buck Rodgers, the former vice president of marketing for IBM, "IBM's goal is to be the low-cost producer, and we have achieved that . . . but that has not distracted us in any way at all from being customer-oriented." IBM in the mid-1980s, he said, is "trying to be a little bit leaner. It's the sort of cycle you go through. I consider it to be a cleansing operation. You have to step back and say, 'What are we spending the dollars on?' and try to make a delineation between what I call desirability and necessity."

☐ At Deere, according to Russ Sutherland, vice president of engineering, "We have found ways to become more effective in manufacturing, including the design process, that allows us to produce products without sacrificing quality as defined by the customer."

☐ At the same time that Xerox is concentrating on improving its customer focus and increasing customer satisfaction, the company is trying to get its costs down to the level of its Japanese competitors. Xerox management doesn't see any contradiction between these two goals. As one of its executives said, "If you give the most accurate service, you will have optimized both the customer and the cost at the same time."

These statements are not just corporate puffery; in the past few years, these companies have made significant investments in reducing their costs. In 1985 IBM spent about $3 billion on improving its manufacturing capabilities and there are plans to spend at least one-third of the capital budget from 1986 to 1989 (about $45 billion) on making its factories highly competitive showcases of manufacturing technology. The result is that today IBM appears to be the low-cost producer of many items, such as printers and other peripherals, where once the Japanese reigned supreme. For a decade (1975 to 1985) Deere single-mindedly poured vast sums of money into modernizing its facilities, cutting marketing and administrative costs, and reducing total employment without massive layoffs. By the decade's end, Deere's break-even volume was estimated to be well below that of its closest competitors. A significant factor in Xerox's mid-1980s resurgence in the market for low-priced copiers was its ability to get its costs down to competitive levels through substantial cost-cutting and improvements in manufacturing efficiency.

### No Paradox

Is theory wrong? Can cost-minimization and keeping customers happy go hand-in-hand? Not really. To understand why this is not a paradox at least three factors must be considered when evaluating the apparent success of these winners:

☐ *Corporate Flab.* Part of the cost gap between these companies and their more efficient, overseas competition resulted from excessive corporate overhead. Reducing this fat didn't hurt customer satisfaction levels at these companies; neither did it make the businesses cost leaders. It merely made them more efficient.

☐ *Technological Investments.* The relationship between customer satisfaction and product costs assumes a particular technology. Using an improved technology, companies can lower their costs while maintaining customer satisfaction. If and when the original cost leader adopts the new technology, however, that company will again be more cost efficient, although still providing less satisfaction. (See Figure 1.1c)

☐ *The Jury's Still Out.* It's too early to tell if these companies have cut just fat or if they've taken away some muscle. Customer satisfaction can change gradually in either direction, so the results of these efforts may not be known until the late 1980s and early 1990s. In this connection IBM's recent experiences in the PC market are not reassuring; despite substantial investments in manufacturing and a highly praised sales organization, the company has lost substantial chunks of its market to competitors, particularly to lower-cost clones.

The basic dichotomy still holds: You can maximize customer satisfaction while keeping costs below a specified level, or you can minimize costs while maintaining a parity level of customer satisfaction. You can't do both.

We believe that what IBM, Deere, Xerox, and others are trying to do is to keep customer satisfaction as high as possible while getting within striking distance of the low-cost providers. Viewed in this light, the previously quoted comments should be taken as symptomatic of the balancing act these executives have to perform, and as exhortations to the troops not to forget costs while they are concentrating on customer satisfaction.

## MOST COMPANIES ARE COST-FOCUSED

Probably not since William Vanderbilt said "the public be damned" has a business executive openly suggested that the customer doesn't matter. However, once we get past the corporate symbols—the mission statements, advertising slogans, inspirational messages, and posters—we find that most companies stress cost, not customers.

How can we be so sure? When push comes to shove, when the question is one of either cutting costs to make the quarterly profit goal or investing to increase customer satisfaction, most companies emphasize cost over the customer.

☐ Buck Rodgers of IBM says one of the reasons some companies fail is that although they may say they want to understand the customer, "When times get tough or they get caught up in mergers or other things, it sort of falls by the wayside. They don't do it on a sustained basis."

☐ Ford's experiences with the E-coat process, described earlier, provide a grim example of this cost focus. Despite the fact that the process had become an industry standard, "Ford itself moved very slowly in installing the process in its American plants. . . . [T]he reluctance of the company to adopt a technique so clearly superior and so critical to basic quality symbolized for many Ford's indifference to quality." The problem, of course, was the cost. It was only in 1984, more than 25 years after Ford had invented the E-coat process, and well after its major competitors had installed it in *their* manufacturing facilities, that the company got it into all of its plants.

Companies choose to minimize costs rather than maximize customer satisfaction for three reasons. First, top management has a short-term orientation that stresses immediate payback on investments. Second, the benefits of a customer-oriented approach are cumulative and become apparent only after a number of years. Third, the intensely competitive atmosphere of the 1970s and 1980s placed additional emphasis on cost-cutting.

1. *Short-Term Orientation.* By and large, senior managers tend to focus almost exclusively on short-term performance—the next quarter, the next six months, or the next fiscal year. There are many reasons, including bonuses tied to annual performance, pressure from Wall Street to show continuous high growth in sales and earnings, and the company's fear of a takeover. This short-term focus is reinforced by the widespread use of the net present value approach to investment decisions, which tends to over-emphasize immediate results and discount or disregard .

long-term benefits. [See, e.g., "Managing our way to economic decline." Abernathy and Hayes, *Harvard Business Review*, July–August 1980, pp. 67–77.]

2. *Cumulative, Long-Term Benefits.* The immediate impact of investments that keep the customer happy is usually very difficult to measure. Such investments are different from capital expenditures on new tooling or product cost reductions. For instance, we cannot say with any certainty that investing $X$ in improving customer service will increase next year's profits by $Y$. Customers do not normally respond to any one activity; instead, their attitudes are conditioned by the cumulative impact of such efforts over an extended period. Swissair, for example, stands out in customer satisfaction because of the years it has spent patiently nurturing its passengers. The company has made steady, sometimes major, investments in cabin crew training, in improving response times at check-in, in maintaining a reputation for punctuality despite higher fuel costs, and so on. It would be impossible to quantify separately the effect of, say, improving counter service on customer satisfaction, nor does Swissair try to do it. Customers keep coming back because they like the total Swissair package.

The combination of these two factors—the short-term orientation of top management and the cumulative, longer-range impact of customer-oriented investments—encourages a cost-minimization strategy. The short-term orientation inexorably makes managers stress immediate payback, aided and abetted by their favorite tool, net present value. The difficulty, if not impossibility, of measuring the effect of customer-oriented investments compounds the problem. Frustrated by their inability to quantify the impact of customer-oriented investments, managers start downplaying the importance of maximizing customer satisfaction. Instead, the functional background of many managers, usually in finance or law or another support activity, training, and the NPV (net present value) criterion combine to make the shift to a cost-minimization strategy logical and virtually inevitable.

3. *Global Competition*. The intensely competitive global market-place of the 1970s and 1980s has reinforced managers' tendencies to be cost-focused. Faced with overseas competitors enjoying substantial labor-cost advantages, many U.S. and European firms have come to view cost-cutting as their only hope of survival. This increased competitiveness and consequent pressure on costs have created the following spiral:

Competitive pressures squeeze market share, profit margins, and cash flow.

At the same time, the need to become cost-competitive results in greater demands on capital for factory automation, new tooling, CAD/CAM, and so on.

Consequently, investments in improving customer satisfaction have to be postponed or even abandoned.

This further reduces the firm's competitive advantage over its foreign counterparts. Customers who find themselves less satisfied, yet often paying higher prices, start abandoning the firm.

As more customers switch, the firm's market share and profits are squeezed further and the cycle repeats itself.

### The Bottom Line

Although a cost-focused approach provides significant short-term rewards, over time it leaves the firm more vulnerable to competition and less profitable. Products that provide parity levels of satisfaction become commodities; customers don't have a reason to stay with a particular brand or manufacturer. Mistakes in judging what constitutes an acceptable level of customer satisfaction create a pool of discontent that rivals can exploit. Finally, focusing exclusively on cost-reduction can back the firm into technologies and investments that become a burden when new developments render these capabilities obsolete.

Henry Ford created the Model T, the first mass-produced car. At the time it was introduced, the car clearly maximized customer satisfaction. Its chassis was high which meant that, unlike fancier cars, it could ride over serious bumps. Unimproved dirt tracks, built for farm horses, created no problems for it. If something went wrong with the car, the average owner could get out and fix it, important in days when there were no service stations and few skilled mechanics. And it was priced at a level the average buyer could afford. By 1922 Ford's sales were over $100 million.

But even as he succeeded in the marketplace, Ford's focus shifted from market needs to manufacturing efficiency, that is, from a customer-focus to a cost-focus. He increasingly believed that all that was necessary to keep customers happy, and buying cars, was to continually cut the price of the car. He thus ignored the major changes that had occurred in the marketplace. The United States' roads were no longer just dirt tracks. Buyers wanted more speed, comfort, and convenience, such things as two front doors instead of one! But Ford's response was entirely negative; to a group of dealers who asked if he could vary the color of the Model T, he replied with the now-famous line, "You can have any color you want, boys, as long as it's black." His reason: Any changes in the car slowed down the production line and raised the cost. The result was inevitable. By 1927 Ford had lost its market leadership to General Motors for the first time, and since 1936, has been unable to regain it.

# 2

# *Customer Satisfaction Creates Market Success*

This is the central premise of the marketing concept: Keeping customers happy is good business. In our research we tested this premise in two different ways. First, we analyzed our winners to determine what benefits, if any, they had obtained by providing superior customer satisfaction. Second, we tried to quantify the relationship between customer satisfaction and such variables as market share and overall profitability.

In both cases our findings confirm that companies don't have to sacrifice profitability to keep customers happy. In fact, quite the reverse is true: Firms that consistently rank high on customer satisfaction also rank high in profitability, as shown by our examples of winners—Swissair, Federal Express Corp., Maytag Co., IBM, Northwestern Mutual Life Insurance Co., Mercedes-Benz, Xerox Corp., and others. Nor was this merely coincidental; each of these companies is convinced that customer satisfaction is a key reason for their superior financial performance.

Our quantitative analyses confirmed these findings. We found that customer loyalty was intimately related to satisfaction with the product. The happier customers are with a given product or service, the more likely they are to buy it again, and the less likely they are to switch to competing products. We were able to identify key factors affecting customer satisfaction and, for the farm equipment industry, we were able to demonstrate a direct relationship between customer satisfaction, market share, and overall profitability.

## THE REASONS WHY

Companies that adopt the strategy of maximizing customer satisfaction obtain several vital competitive advantages. Their long-term profitability is normally higher than their competitors', they have more protection against shifts in technology and customers' needs, and if they should slip up, their chances of regaining lost customers and markets are better.

### Higher Long-Term Profitability

By providing superior customer satisfaction, the company obtains several competitive advantages that lead to higher profitability.

1. *Less Wasted Motion.* In the process of keeping customers happy, the company gets to know them so well that it makes fewer false starts. The firm often knows what customers want even before they are aware of it. This allows the company to anticipate customer needs and wants and move into position economically and early. It doesn't need to spend time and money on fruitless market research surveys or false starts in new product development. It just *knows*! Charles Revson, the legendary

founder of Revlon, wasted very little time or money on customer surveys and test marketing; he had an uncanny ability to pick colors, shades, and packages that women would like. Mercedes-Benz similarly knows that its customers want functional, not plush, cars. Therefore it resists excessive gadgetry and frequent changes in styling.

2. *The Firm Gets a Price Advantage.* In industry after industry, happy customers are willing to pay extra for the additional satisfaction they derive. How much extra? That depends on other factors such as the overall competitive environment, the price sensitivity of customers, the type of purchase, and company positioning. However, be it small or large, that extra margin is always there. Federal Express consistently gets a somewhat higher price for its overnight delivery service than does the competition. Maytag has always commanded a substantial premium for its products as compared with its industry rivals, Whirlpool and GE. Swissair's revenue per passenger mile is usually a bit higher than that of its rivals, as is the revenue per passenger mile of Delta in the United States. In the good years, farmers paid as much as 15 percent more to buy a Deere product; even in today's difficult farm economy, Deere's equipment still gets a premium, although not 15 percent. Mercedes-Benz, which is also a world-class manufacturer of trucks, gets a price premium from tight-fisted Third World buyers for its trucks as well as its cars. Firms in industries such as packaged goods may not be able to command a premium price. Yet they often benefit by avoiding the necessity of offering discount coupons, free gifts, special promotions, and the like.

3. *Customers Come Back More Often.* Satisfied customers are more loyal to their brands than are dissatisfied customers. They're more likely to come back to the company's products and to buy other products the company makes. Combined with their willingness to pay a price premium, this higher repeat rate leads to greater revenues and, ultimately, more profits. This is particularly valuable in a highly competitive industry where the price pre-

mium may be tiny—1 to 5 percent at best—as is often the case in packaged goods, some consumer durables and various services. In such situations, the slight price advantage, together with the higher loyalty or repeat rate, slowly but steadily adds up to greater long-term profitability.

4. *Transaction Costs Are Lower.* As every salesperson knows, it is easier to make a repeat sale than it is to open new accounts. Thus greater customer loyalty means that the company's continuing sales expenses are lower. The firm doesn't have to spend as much time persuading the customer to buy its products. The question is no longer why the customer should buy the company's products. Instead, the focus is on which products, and how much, the customer should buy. In many cases, the salesperson merely takes the order and answers customer's questions; the salesperson doesn't have to spend a lot of time selling. In addition, credit approval, order processing, shipping, and other transaction costs are lower, since the preliminary paperwork has been done and the pertinent information about the customer has been entered and verified. Those savings add up to a tangible cost advantage.

5. *Communications Costs Are Lower.* Happy customers act like a volunteer salesforce; they tell others—friends, relatives, neighboring businesses, and so forth. According to Harvey Lamm, president of Subaru of America, Inc., customer satisfaction was Subaru's primary source of advertising when they first began marketing in the United States. "The domestics have a very high level of awareness. They have almost catastrophic budgets allocated to advertising and brand identification—and we had none. We had no financial support and we had no line of business to generate those dollars. From the beginning, out of pure necessity, we had to develop a program, a marketing concept that would build on referral . . . [and] without the satisfaction of the customer, the referral is impossible." Studies show that such word-of-mouth advertising is also far more effective than other means of communicating with customers. Thus the firm gets a double benefit: Its communications are both less expensive and more ef-

fective than the competition's. Subaru, for example, spends less per car on advertising than its counterparts, for the simple reason that word-of-mouth recommendations are still its strongest sales generators.

### Better Protected from Competitors

Not only are happy customers more loyal, they stay more loyal longer. They're less likely to jump to new products, or to abandon their traditional supplier for a new one whose products are somewhat cheaper. This gives the firm a breathing space, a grace period that, used wisely, can help protect the firm from competitive inroads.

1. *Customers Don't Jump Immediately to a New Product.* IBM was late to enter the microcomputer market, coming out with its first PC five years after Apple launched the Apple II. Yet IBM's customers, the larger corporate buyers, waited patiently. There were no defections, of any consequence, to Apple. Nor was this an isolated occurrence; in several instances IBM has been slow to enter a new area, yet has managed to become the leader because its customers were loyal.

2. *Customers Don't Switch at Once to a Lower-Priced Entrant.* Just as happy customers are willing to pay a little more, they're also less likely to switch when a new entrant comes in with lower prices. For example, Caterpillar Tractor's U.S. customers stayed loyal when Komatsu entered the market, even though the price difference was as high as 20 to 30 percent. This gave Caterpillar time to make the investments necessary to close the price gap. Kodak has held on to 85 percent of the market for photographic film, despite aggressive price competition from Fuji. Compaq has been shielded from PC-compatible imports because it has kept its customers—computer retailers—very happy. Of course, nothing is forever; customers do not stay loyal when the price differences become acute. Because IBM was slow to react when cutting the

prices of its PCs in response to competition, it has lost a substantial portion of this market to clones and imports.

### Better Protected Against Shifts in Customer Needs

Maximizing customer satisfaction also gives the firm time to react to changes in customer needs. This is true for two reasons: The firm is able to anticipate such shifts, and customers will wait for the company to make the transition. Swissair was slow to adjust to the new international travel environment, being late in introducing business class, frequent-flier programs, and wider-spaced seating in first class. Yet its passengers stayed with the airline, all the while providing abundant feedback about the need to change. Deere's sensitivity to large farmers' needs allowed it to anticipate the mid-1960s shift to fewer, larger farms, more horsepower, and better parts and service support. In its major markets—homes, educational institutions, and small businesses—Apple is still the major player, despite the shift to an IBM standard in the corporate world.

### Able To Regain Lost Markets

Even loyal customers don't wait forever. If a company is too slow, obtuse, short-sighted, or unwilling to change, customers will switch to alternative suppliers. However, there is often a reservoir of goodwill that allows the firm to make a successful comeback. It's almost as though customers were saying, "We're glad you finally understand what we'd like you to do. Welcome back to the fold!"

☐ Prior to 1980, very few Jaguar customers were willing even to acknowledge they owned the car, so poor was its reputation for quality and reliability. But deep down, they loved the Jaguar's styling and performance. Thus, as soon as they became convinced that the company was mending its ways, they came running back. Jaguar's sales in the United States, its largest market, went from 3,021 cars in 1980 to 20,528 in 1985.

☐ Xerox is slowly regaining market share it lost to the Japanese. From 1983 to 1985 its share of the market, in terms of units sold and net rental additions, has increased from 23.3 to 30.3 percent.

## ANALYZING THE RELATIONSHIP

While our research into individual firms provided us with valuable information about how they achieved superior customer satisfaction, these data were, of necessity, qualitative. They could not provide answers to such questions as, "How much additional profit can a firm expect to make if it keeps its customers happy? What is the exact relationship between customer satisfaction and market share? Does increasing customer satisfaction by $X$ percent mean that loyalty will increase by $Y$ percent?"

To some extent, these issues have been studied by other researchers. For example, on the basis of data submitted by over 1000 corporate participants, the PIMS (Profit Impact of Market Share) project at the Harvard Business School found that firms providing superior product quality also had superior financial performance (Figure 2.1). Superior product quality is usually closely related to superior customer satisfaction; by extension, then, superior customer satisfaction leads to higher profitability.

We decided to study these relationships in more detail to see whether we could identify any broad patterns. We focused on the passenger airline, farm equipment, and automobile industries. Our main reason for choosing these three industries was the ready availability of information about customer satisfaction and

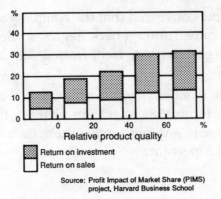

Source: Profit Impact of Market Share (PIMS)
project, Harvard Business School

*Figure 2.1 Profitability increases with relative product quality*

financial performance. In addition, these three industries exhibit a wide variation in the external factors that affect the relationship between customer satisfaction and profitability:

1. *Information Available to the Buyer.* Other things being equal, the more information customers have or can obtain easily prior to purchase, the more knowledgeable they will be. In turn, the more knowledgeable the customers, the more likely that they will choose products and services that maximize satisfaction. Consequently the more likely it is that firms that keep customers happy will show superior financial performance. Airline passengers have relatively little information regarding the performance of the various carriers. Farmers, on the other hand, are extremely knowledgeable about the relative merits of the different makes of equipment, while car buyers fall somewhere in the middle.

2. *Nature of the Purchase.* We would expect that one-time or infrequent purchases would be least influenced by considerations of customer satisfaction, while repeat purchases and industrial buying decisions would be heavily influenced by these factors. Vacation travel represents a one-time or infrequent purchase while farm equipment is an example of an industrial buying decision. Car purchases fall somewhere in the middle. They are repeat purchases and are a major decision. On the other hand, in

car purchases, subjective factors such as styling, color, and interior comfort play a much greater role, with the result that customer satisfaction may have less of an impact than in the case of farm equipment.

3. *Degree of Price Sensitivity.* We would expect that the more price sensitive the customers are the less influence overall satisfaction will have on their decisions. Vacation travelers are very price conscious; business travelers are less so. Car buyers' sensitivity to price varies by demographic segment and the type of car being purchased; other things being equal, a compact car buyer is much more likely to be influenced by price than someone in the market for a luxury sedan. Farmers are affected by price, but they also weigh the total life-cycle cost including the likely trade-in value.

4. *Duration of Postsales Support Needs.* Other things being equal, the more after-sales support buyers need, the more likely their satisfaction with the product will influence their decisions. Airline trips are essentially a consumption item; there is very little after-sales support needed and, therefore, few travelers select an airline on this basis. Farm equipment is at the other extreme, requiring considerable after-sales service and parts support. Automobiles fall somewhere in the middle; after-sales support is important, but is widely available; consequently it is not as important an influence on consumer choices as compared to, say, styling and availability.

### What We Found

For each industry we obtained customer satisfaction, profitability, and market share data for the several companies active in the industry. We then analyzed this information to see if we could identify any patterns that would show a clear link between customer satisfaction and success in the marketplace.

As might be expected, our results were mixed. The relationship between customer satisfaction and financial performance was weakest in the airline industry, and strongest in farm equipment. In the automotive industry we found a very close relationship between customer satisfaction and the likelihood that they would buy the same make of car again. With the help of this relationship we could successfully explain the various changes in the market, such as the continued growth in the sales of Japanese and selected European imports and the reasons for General Motors' loss of market share. However, it was difficult to relate customer satisfaction directly to the financial performance of individual firms.

These results were not a surprise. In the airline industry a large number of factors other than overall satisfaction influence the choice of a particular carrier. Consequently we would expect the relationship between customer satisfaction and market success to be weak. Farm equipment is at the opposite extreme; all the external factors—the amount of information buyers have, the nature of the purchase, the relative importance of price, after-sales support requirements—act to strengthen the link between customer satisfaction and profitability. Then, as one might expect, the car industry is in the middle. How happy owners are with their car definitely affects their future intentions. However, because of the long time interval between purchases, owners may not always follow their stated intentions; a better price, an appealing style, the ready availability of a particular model on the lot—such factors may cause them to buy a different make that may not be as satisfying.

## THE AIRLINE INDUSTRY

We analyzed both domestic and international airlines. For the domestic airlines we used the number of complaints filed with the Civil Aeronautics Board for every thousand passengers as a measure of customer satisfaction. These statistics were available for a number of years and they appeared to track reasonably well with independent surveys of customer satisfaction. We reviewed financial performance over the years 1975–1985. Airline deregulation occurred in 1980; thus this period covers both pre- and post-deregulation performance. For the international carriers, we used passenger surveys conducted by International Travel News, in Sacramento, California. In 1982 and 1985 this organization surveyed a large number of airline passengers regarding their satisfaction with various airlines, both foreign and domestic. The financial data were obtained from various published sources.

We didn't find an overall relationship linking customer satisfaction with market success. However, we did find several cases where we observed a definite pattern connecting the two variables.

### Delta versus Eastern

Delta and Eastern Airlines provide an excellent pair of case studies for understanding how customer satisfaction can affect financial performance. For several decades these two airlines have served overlapping markets for air travel in the eastern and southeastern United States. Eastern has had many advantages in its favor: It grew rapidly in the regulated era to become the nation's largest carrier in terms of number of passengers carried and also had many lucrative, high-volume routes, including the East Coast shuttle and the run from New York to Florida.

However, over the past 10 years Delta has been by far the more profitable airline. Eastern, on the other hand, spent years staggering from one financial crisis to another, until it was finally taken over by Frank Lorenzo.

Although a number of factors such as intransigent unions, the advent of jet aircraft which changed the economics of Eastern's route structure, and airline deregulation definitely affected the outcome, one fact stands out: Eastern was never able to create a strong, loyal group of customers that would enable it to recover from its mistakes.

While Delta has always had the lowest number of complaints per thousand among the major airlines, Eastern has usually been among the highest. This is no surprise to seasoned travelers among whom Eastern has long been notorious for its erratic and often downright poor customer relations.

Nor is this a coincidence. Delta has had a conscious, customer-oriented strategy. From the beginning, the firm appears to have been customer-focused. This is evident in every aspect of its strategy. The company was a pioneer in the "hub-and-spoke" system, which provides frequent departures without raising operating costs. Delta realized that punctuality and timely baggage delivery were critical to customer satisfaction and made certain that it delivered. Since an airline's employees are the key to delivering high levels of satisfaction, Delta has made superior employee relations an important corporate goal. Alone among the major airlines, Delta is largely nonunion and has a no-layoff policy. In turn, this has permitted a remarkable degree of flexibility; at Delta, there are no union work rules. Every employee performs several functions. Further, top management has consistently communicated its focus on the customer and its dedication to teamwork in many ways, large and small. For example, during the busy Christmas season, Delta's corporate officers pitch in to help with the baggage. Delta's performance, like its slogan, "Delta gets you there," is not jazzy but is focused on satisfaction.

By contrast, Eastern lacked a coherent strategy. Its approach, like its customer relations, was highly erratic. It would be nice to say that, in contrast to Delta, Eastern concentrated on minimizing costs; unfortunately, even that's not true. Eastern's labor relations were always contentious. Its costs were among the highest of the major trunk air carriers. Despite public statements by its management and sustained efforts over the past few years to improve customer relations, Eastern's record didn't improve until finally this once-proud airline, one of the pioneers of air travel, ceased to exist.

The real difference became glaringly evident after the airlines were deregulated in 1979 (Figure 2.2). Although all major carriers suffered during the 1982 recession, Delta's revenue per passenger mile increased while that of the industry and Eastern stagnated. Both came under attack from low-fare, nonunion start-ups such as People Express and New York Air. Yet overall, Delta has outperformed both the industry and Eastern in net income as a percent of operating revenue (Figure 2.3). Even more telling has been the average revenue per passenger mile: approximately 15 percent for Delta versus 13 percent for Eastern. Therefore we must conclude;

> Eastern survived under regulatory protections and, once they were gone, customers voted with their feet by switching to other airlines;
>
> Despite carrying a larger number of passengers, Eastern could not create a loyal base of customers while Delta could and did;
>
> Delta's investments in customer satisfaction paid off under

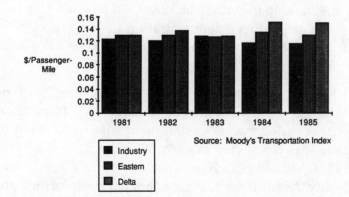

*Figure 2.2 Airline revenues per passenger-mile*

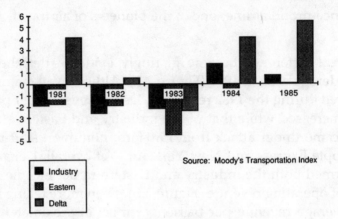

*Figure 2.3 Airline net after-tax income as percent of operating revenue*

deregulation—the airline held on to most of its passengers and probably gained some from Eastern.

## FARM EQUIPMENT

Farm equipment—tractors, combines, tillage and cultivating equipment, and other agricultural implements—offers a distinct contrast to the airline industry. There are only a handful of major firms in the industry. The buyers are highly knowledgeable and they are not making impulse purchases. As a result, this industry provides the most direct demonstration of the proposition that customer satisfaction and financial performance are closely related.

We studied the relationship between satisfaction and performance with the help of a survey of over 1200 farmers, representing every major make of equipment sold in North America. This survey was conducted in early 1983; we have used this data because (1) it was extremely comprehensive and reliable and (2) subsequently the industry has consolidated even further, making a similar analysis virtually meaningless.

The results of this survey showed a very direct link between cus-

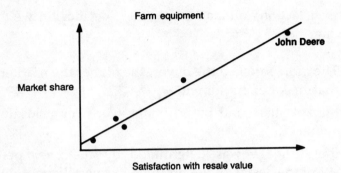

*Figure 2.4 Greater satisfaction leads to greater market share*

Brand image was determined, we found, by the buyers' perceptions regarding the companies' design and engineering, the quality of their dealer networks, the overall quality of the products,
their responsiveness in the event of product problems and, of
course, resale value. This confirmed our expectations about how
farmers purchase equipment; they are very well informed about
the performance of the various makes, and are not influenced ex-
cessively by any one factor, such as special features or heavy advertising.

### Share and Loyalty

Happy customers *are* more loyal; this was confirmed when we
plotted the customers' propensity to switch against their satisfaction levels. Once again, Deere customers, who ranked highest in
satisfaction, were least likely to switch. On the other hand, almost
half the customers of the low-share brands indicated a willingness, even a desire to switch.

## U.S. AUTOMOBILE INDUSTRY

We found the same close relationship between customer satisfaction and loyalty in this industry. The happier the buyers, the

tomer satisfaction and market success. Specifically, we found t
following:

☐ The more satisfied the buyer, the higher the market share
that make of equipment.

☐ Market share and brand image were very closely tied
gether.

☐ Brand image was determined by customer perceptic
about the design of the product, its overall quality, the aft
sales support, and its likely resale value.

☐ Dissatisfied customers were far more likely to switch brar
than satisfied ones.

## Satisfaction and Share

One of the most revealing measures of farmers' true feeli
about a particular make of equipment is how satisfied they
with its resale value. The reason is simple. A well-designed p
of equipment that is easy to use, has proven reliability and d
bility, and has been well supported by the dealer organizatio
worth a lot more than one that falls short in any of these ar
When we plotted farmers' satisfaction with resale value aga
the market share of individual brands, we found a remark;
close relationship (Figure 2.4). Deere buyers were the most
isfied with the resale value and it was the share leader. Purc
ers of other makes were far less satisfied and their market sh
were correspondingly far lower.

## Share and Brand Image

These findings were abundantly confirmed when we analy
how farmers perceived various makes and how these percept
correlated with market share. Deere was perceived as the "b
brand, followed by the rest, and the market shares of indivic
firms were tied very closely to these perceptions.

more likely they were to purchase that particular make of car in the future. However, we could not relate customer satisfaction directly to market share or profitability for several reasons: First, it was impossible to measure the financial performance of individual nameplates, for example, Chevrolet or Plymouth. Second, industry profitability is affected by a number of other factors such as overall capacity utilization, unit labor costs, exchange rates, and, for the period beginning in 1982, the voluntary import restraints observed by Japanese manufacturers. In addition, car buyers have less information as compared with farmers; consequently there is more variation in their actual choices. For this reason market share is not directly related to customer satisfaction. What we did find, however, were broad patterns that correspond very well to the commercial successes (and failures) of individual manufacturers.

Our main sources of data regarding customer satisfaction were the surveys carried out by J.D. Power and Associates of Westlake Village, California. Since 1981, this market research firm has conducted annual surveys of car owners, measuring their satisfaction with various aspects of car ownership, such as condition at the time of delivery, dealership attitude, dealership sales and service personnel, and vehicle reliability. With the help of these surveys, the firm has created a customer satisfaction index which is now widely reported and used within the industry. These surveys are quite extensive; for example, the 1986 survey obtained the views of over 20,000 car owners of 1985 model cars representing 29 major nameplates: 12 domestic and 17 imports.

### Satisfaction and Loyalty

When we compared the percentage of favorable responses to the question, "How likely would you be to purchase this same *make* if you were to replace this car with another?" with the percentage of customers who declared themselves "very satisfied" with their

car, the results were highly revealing and, for U.S. car manufacturers, disturbing (Figure 2.5).

☐ The more satisfied the car buyers, the more likely that they
   will purchase the same make again.

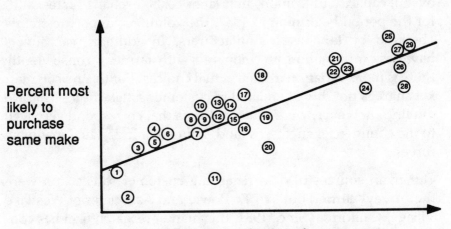

Figure 2.5 lists the makes of automobiles:

## Makes of automobiles

| | | | |
|---|---|---|---|
| 1 | Peugeot | 16 | Volkswagon |
| 2 | AMC/Renault | 17 | BMW |
| 3 | Plymouth | 18 | Lincoln |
| 4 | Pontiac | 19 | Nissan |
| 5 | Dodge | 20 | Mitsubishi |
| 6 | Chevrolet | 21 | Porsche |
| 7 | Alpha Romeo | 22 | Volvo |
| 8 | Chrysler | 23 | Saab |
| 9 | Ford | 24 | Subaru |
| 10 | Cadillac | 25 | Mercedes-Benz |
| 11 | Isuzu | 26 | Honda |
| 12 | Mercury | 27 | Jaguar |
| 13 | Oldsmobile | 28 | Mazda |
| 14 | Buick | 29 | Toyota |
| 15 | Audi | | |

*Figure 2.5 Overall satisfaction leads to greater loyalty*

☐ There appeared to be two distinct groups of makes: a top group in which more than *two-thirds* of the buyers considered themselves "very satisfied," and the rest.

☐ Four out of the six major Japanese car makes were part of the top group, as were five European imports.

☐ Not one U.S. nameplate made it into the top group. Lincoln rated highest, with approximately 58 percent of Lincoln buyers expressing themselves "very satisfied"; for Mercedes-Benz the corresponding figure was 75 percent.

☐ Neither Volkswagen nor Nissan (Datsun) made it into the top group.

☐ Chevrolet and Pontiac were in the lowest 20th percentile in customer satisfaction.

To appreciate fully the implications of this data, assume that Toyota and Chevrolet each start out with 100 car owners apiece and that each owner keeps the car an average of three years before replacing it. Then after nine years (three purchases) Chevrolet will have lost almost 90 of its customers, while Toyota will have lost only 60. The reason? According to the survey, at any time only 47 percent of Chevrolet owners plan to buy another Chevy, whereas 73 percent of Toyota owners will stay loyal to Toyota. On this basis, if we started out in Year 1 with 100 owners apiece, in Year 3 the number of Chevy owners would be 47, while 73 people would own Toyotas. In Year 6, there would be only 22 (47 × 0.47) Chevy owners and 54 (73 × 0.73) Toyota owners and in Year 9 there would be 10 customers owning Chevrolets and almost 40 owning Toyotas.

This analysis is highly simplified; it ignores such things as the possibility that some former Chevy owners will switch back or that Chevy will gain sales from owners of other (non-Toyota) makes switching to Chevy. However, it does help explain why General Motors is losing market share; why Nissan and Volkswagen are falling behind; why U.S. manufacturers will find it extremely difficult to recover the ground lost to companies like Toyota and Subaru, and why Mercedes-Benz continues its growth despite high prices.

### Factors Affecting Customer Satisfaction

A major, almost overwhelming influence on customer satisfaction is how satisfied customers are with their new cars. If customers are happy with the new car as delivered, if there are no squeaks, rattles, or other problems, then the odds are excellent that they will live happily ever after with the car (Figure 2.6). Further, there is a difference between domestics and imports; the relationship between new car and overall satisfaction is much more pronounced in the case of imports.

On the other hand, satisfaction with the dealer has considerably more impact on overall satisfaction in the case of domestic makes; for imports, the effect is much weaker. This suggests that Detroit's dealer network, which should have been a major deterrent to imports, is no longer effective; there is little to choose between the two groups of customers in terms of their satisfaction with their dealer. On the contrary, Detroit's well-known problems with "fits and finishes" when combined with the fact that satis-

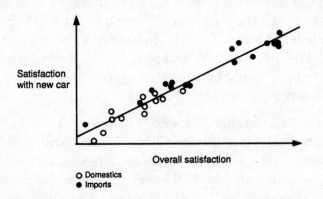

Figure 2.6 Satisfaction with new product leads to greater overall satisfaction

faction with the dealer has a very strong influence on overall satisfaction in the case of domestic cars may actually be exacerbating the problem. Any mistakes by the dealer in preparing the car have much greater impact on customer satisfaction with domestic makes compared with the same mistakes in the case of imported cars, where the influence of satisfaction with the dealer on overall satisfaction is negligible.

These findings graphically demonstrate the reason for the continued success of imports, especially Japanese imports: Customers *like* these cars and they like them more than they like Detroit's products, often much more. While a certain number of customers continue to purchase domestic cars, they're more willing to switch than are purchasers of imports. Thus GM, Ford, and Chrysler will, in all probability, lose more customers to imports than they will capture from the imports! Consequently, there is little reason to believe that the market share of imports will stop growing in the near future, especially when we consider that people are keeping their cars longer, meaning that there are fewer opportunities for domestic car makers to persuade customers to switch back. What is more, the substantially higher levels of satisfaction with imports indicate that a weaker dollar (and therefore higher prices for imports) is not likely to have an effect in the near future. Customers who like a Toyota almost twice as much as a Chevrolet probably won't switch until the Toyota costs a lot more (perhaps as much as 50 percent more) than the Chevy.

# 3

# How the Winners Do It

## THE CHARACTERISTICS
## OF SUCCESS

*Federal Express has been known to deliver a single package via Lear jet to keep a promise to a customer.*

*Six Flags broadcasts "busy-day alerts" to warn customers that they're likely to encounter crowds and traffic jams on their way to the amusement park.*

*Swissair asks thousands of passengers several times each year what they think of the airline, and isn't satisfied with an approval rating of less than 96 percent.*

Sounds crazy, doesn't it? Spend thousands of dollars to deliver one $14.00 package? Turn customers away and tell them not to come today? Ninety-six percent, that's impossible! What's wrong with 90 percent? Is that how these companies keep their customers happy, by throwing money at them? How long can they expect to remain profitable if they carry on like this?

Federal Express, Six Flags, and Swissair are not charitable organizations. Nor do they throw money at customer problems. What's more, they have been profitable for a long time and fully intend to stay that way. Yet they, and other companies like them, continue to do these "crazy" things because they know that *their profits come from keeping customers happy.*

Everyone in business pays lip service to the importance of keeping customers happy. We have all seen slogans like "Customers make paydays possible," "The customer is king," and "We are a customer-driven organization." Yet in most industries only one or two firms manage to put these noble sentiments into action. What makes these companies tick? How can they afford to spend the additional time and money needed to try and keep *every* customer happy and still remain profitable? Is it accidental or part of their grand design? What techniques do they use?

We decided that the best way to find the answer was to ask the companies. We wanted to study them closely, with their cooperation, and discover for ourselves the depth of their apparent commitment to customers, the reasons that led these firms to become customer focused, and the tools and techniques they used to achieve this objective.

## HOW WE RESEARCHED THE WINNERS

The first step was identifying the winners. First and foremost, we were looking for firms that were industry leaders in *both* customer satisfaction and long-term financial performance. To this basic requirement we added two further criteria:

1. We wanted to study firms in as many different industries as possible.
2. We wanted a cross-section of managerial styles, growth patterns, and internal cultures.

While financial information was readily available, finding out which companies really provided superior customer satisfaction (as opposed to claiming merely that they did) proved to be a challenge. In some industries it was very clear-cut. Independent measurements of customer satisfaction were readily available and it was immediately obvious who the winners were. In other cases, where such information was lacking, we had to rely on business and trade publications, industry experts, and personal knowledge.

We finally selected 15 firms in 13 different industries, covering everything from aerospace to residential real estate (see Table 3.1). Structurally the industries in which these firms operated were very diverse, from fragmented (real estate, insurance, air travel) to extremely concentrated (farm equipment, commercial aircraft). The prices of their products or services ranged from a few dollars (film, amusement parks) to thousands or even millions of dollars (life insurance, commercial aircraft). Competition ranged from low to intense as did the price sensitivity of the buyers. Six of the 15 firms were overall market share leaders while some of the others were leaders in their individual segments. All of them commanded some degree of price premium for their products. Last, each was a leader in customer satisfaction and long-term financial performance.

Of course, these are not the only winners. We identified a number of other firms that also excelled in customer satisfaction and overall profitability: McDonald's in fast food; The Limited in retailing; Migros, the Swiss supermarket chain; Hewlett-Packard and Digital Equipment in computers; Delta Airlines in domestic

TABLE 3.1  *Profile of the Winners*

| Firm | Industry | Competitive Situation | |
|---|---|---|---|
| | | Intensity | Price Sensitivity |
| Mercedes-Benz of North America | Automobile | Medium | Low |
| Subaru | Automobile | Medium–high | Medium |
| Jaguar | Automobile | Medium | Low |
| Boeing Commercial Aircraft Company | Aerospace | Very high | High |
| Federal Express | Overnight delivery | Medium–high | Low |
| Northwestern Mutual Life Insurance | Insurance | Medium | Low-medium |
| Kraft Foodservice | Food distribution | Medium | High |
| Xerox | Office equipment | High | Medium |
| Kodak | Film<br>Office equipment | Medium<br>High | Low<br>Medium |
| Swissair | Passenger airline | High | Medium |
| Deere & Company | Farm equipment | Very high | High |
| Century 21 | Real estate services | Low | Low |
| IBM | Computer and office equipment | Low–high | High–low |
| Maytag | Home laundry equipment | High | Medium |
| Six Flags | Recreation | Low | Low |

| Market Performance | | Customer Satisfaction | |
| --- | --- | --- | --- |
| Share Position | Price Premium | How Determined | Rank |
| 2* | High | J.D. Power and Associates; *Consumer Reports* | 1 |
| 6* | Medium | J.D. Power and Associates; *Consumer Reports* | 2 |
| 4 or 5* | Medium–low | J.D. Power and Associates; *Consumer Reports* | 6 |
| 1 | Some | Industry experts | N/A |
| 1 | Some | Industry experts | N/A |
| 10 | | *Consumer Reports; Fortune* | 1 |
| 3 | Some | Customer surveys | 1 |
| 1* | Some | Customer surveys | 1 |
| 1 | Some | Industry experts | N/A |
| 2* | Some | Customer surveys | |
| N/A | Some | Customer surveys | 1 |
| 1 | Some | Customer surveys | 1 |
| 1 | N/A | Industry experts | N/A |
| 1 | Medium–high | Customer surveys | 1 |
| 2 or 3 | Medium–high | *Consumer Reports; Appliance Magazine* | 1 |
| N/A | Some | Trade opinion | N/A |

air travel; and many others. However, limitations of time and budget prevented us from including these and other winners in our sample.

### Survey Design

Before starting the interviews, we prepared a short survey instrument along the lines shown in Appendix 1 which we forwarded to the firms prior to our meetings with their executives. This allowed the firms to gather necessary data and to ensure that we would be meeting with the managers most concerned with specific issues.

The executives we interviewed held a number of job titles and responsibilities. Among those who participated were chief executive officers; company presidents; vice presidents of operations, marketing, and quality programs; managers of customer service, product evaluation, and consumer relations; and product engineers. Our interviews, sometimes conducted in groups and sometimes with individual executives, generally lasted several hours each. We tape recorded most of these interviews, with the prior knowledge and approval of the interviewees. This permitted free-ranging discussions without the distraction of taking notes. These companies also provided us with follow-up information. In several instances this included details of internal standards, policies and procedures, performance measurements, and analyses of problems. The entire process took nearly two years, from late 1984 until late 1986.

### Interview Focus

First and foremost, we wanted to probe the depth of the firm's commitment to the customer. Specifically, we wanted to know

How important, *in their opinion*, was the role of customer satisfaction in the firm's success?

What specific actions had the firm taken to provide superior customer satisfaction?

What had been the measurable results of these actions?

We were particularly interested in how these companies behaved "at the margin." In other words, did they stick to their beliefs about the customer and make long-term investments even at the risk of a short-term "hit"? Or did they cut and run, like any cost-oriented company would? For this reason we pushed to get case histories about such decisions (i.e., times, places, amounts, people, results). We also held several lengthy discussions with senior managers about "cost versus customer" issues to learn how these practitioners viewed the trade-off and how they resolved it in practice. These discussions gave us invaluable insights into the firms' beliefs and culture.

In addition, we probed into specific areas—product design, quality control, sales attitudes and practices, after-sales support, complaint handling—to learn more about the mechanics: How had the winners managed to design products that provided superior satisfaction? How had they motivated the salesforce or dealers to create a partnership with the customer? What role did after-sales support play in keeping customers happy? How had these firms created the right corporate culture? What incentives did they use? How did they reinforce these values?

## WHAT WE DISCOVERED

Without exception, every one of our winners is convinced that their ability to keep customers happy is *the* key to their continued growth and success. Everyone we talked to in these companies, from the chief executive officer down to operating managers and workers, realized that customer satisfaction was the base on which companies build profitable operations. Most of our winners had always been aware of the importance of customer satisfaction for their profitability. Two companies, Xerox and Jaguar, freely conceded that they had lost sight of this fundamental relationship and traced their recent revivals to new management which has refocused everyone's attention on customer satisfaction again. The following quotes were typical:

We are convinced that Swissair can maintain its position in a competitive market if it offers its customers in the air and on the ground outstanding service in keeping with the traditions of Swiss hospitality. (M. Jaquiery, vice chairman of Swissair)

In 1983 and [in] 1985, we were recognized [by the industry] as the top supplier of the year. I guess if you would go back, into the early 1980s, if they would have given an award for the worst [Kraft] would probably have gotten it. . . . Why? Because we didn't really pay attention to what the customer's needs were. We were so busy running our own business and trying to get our business on stream that we took our focus off the customer and spent all of our time on operating results. And until we really sat down and tried to understand what the customer demands were in this industry, we really were not that successful. (R. Dean Nelson, president of Kraft Foodservice)

We have three major corporate objectives. One is return on assets, another is market share, and third is customer satisfaction. . . . I like to think that "customer" is the base of that triangle, not just because it's the longest word, but because without your customer base, you have neither one of these. (Kerney Laday, vice president of National Service, Xerox)

Our growth, not just in size but financially, has been supported by the fact that our customer base views satisfaction [that we provide as being high]. It's one-third of the process, the very, very important part, customer satisfaction. The other two pieces to the puzzle to our corporate philosophy are people and profits. It's the corporate philosophy that the company grew up with and is embedded deeply in every employee that works at Federal Express. That is, people, service, profits. (Robert Hernandez, vice president of Customer Service, Federal Express)

Customer service is very important. Northwestern prides itself on good persistency—to oversimplify, a measure of repeat business. Better persistency lowers our costs, which increases the value for existing policyowners, which creates more satisfied customers who come back for more business, further lowering our costs, and so forth. (Robert W. Ninneman, senior vice president of Operations, Northwestern Mutual Life Insurance Co.)

Other companies echoed these sentiments. In every case the basic message was the same: Improving customer satisfaction is at the heart of our firm's growth and profitability.

### Customer, Not Cost

These companies' actions confirm this commitment to customer satisfaction. At the margin these companies are definitely customer-focused. Federal Express' willingness to charter a jet for a single package, Six Flags' busy day alerts—these were just two of many such examples of their emphasis on customer satisfaction *even if it meant additional costs*. Xerox delayed the introduction of a badly needed new copier model until it was sure that it met the firm's reliability goals. Deere accepted smaller margins on some equipment rather than sacrifice quality. Maytag cut back its production rather than ship washers with inferior steel. Swissair spends more on fuel to ensure that its planes arrive and leave on time.

When we asked, "How do you resolve the trade-off between cost cutting and investing in customer satisfaction?" with almost monotonous regularity the answer was, "We don't even think of it that way. There is no question of doing trade-off analyses. If we do what's right for the customer, we know that it will pay off in the long run."

Initially we were extremely skeptical; it sounded too good to be true. But when we researched deeper we found ample confirmation. Nowhere did we observe any explicit trade-offs or any evidence of an attitude that said, "If we provide X percent less customer satisfaction, we can save Y percent in costs." Quite the opposite, the investments these firms have made and continue to make, the manner in which they design their products and services, their internal measurement systems and incentives—everything bore witness to management's claim.

How then do they balance these conflicting requirements? By putting the customer first and profitability second, by avoiding explicit trade-offs between customer and cost, and by taking a long-term view. Putting the customer first corrects any bias toward short-term cost savings at the expense of (long-term) customer satisfaction. This is reinforced by avoiding explicit cost trade-offs, which often serve to weaken the firm's commitment to keeping the customer happy. Finally, the long-term approach puts the right perspective on any unavoidable conflicts that occur when considering major investments to improve customer satisfaction.

These firms have instinctively avoided the "soft opinions versus hard facts" debate that occurs in cost-focused firms. Intuitively our winners know that such a debate loads the dice against making long-term investments in keeping customers happy. They also know through experience that quantifying the benefits of a given investment is a difficult, often fruitless, and, possibly, divisive task. Therefore, they prefer to change the focus from "should we do it" to "how do we fund it." Intangibles such as corporate culture, shared values, a cross-functional exposure to and understanding of customer needs, and top management familiarity with customers are relied on to provide the necessary balance between service and cost.

## SIX KEY CHARACTERISTICS

The specific approach taken by each of these firms to make their organization customer-focused varies considerably, reflecting the diversity of their products and services, customers, sales practices and techniques, corporate cultures and managerial styles, and so forth. Xerox is extremely systematic and highly formal, using contracts between individual departments. Deere, on the other hand, is more relaxed and informal. Swissair maintains extensive statistics regarding customers' expectations and its own performance, while Mercedes-Benz combines extensive statistics with a more intuitive approach. Federal Express is quite passionate about the importance of keeping the customer happy; Kodak is more low key about it.

Despite this diversity, the following six characteristics are shared by all our winners and help explain their success in implementing the marketing concept:

1. They set themselves "impossibly high" standards.
2. They're obsessive about knowing, even better than the customers themselves, what the customers want.
3. They create and manage customers' expectations.
4. They design their products or services to maximize customer satisfaction.
5. They put their money where their mouth is.
6. They make customer satisfaction everybody's business.

This commonality was so strong to be almost eerie; sometimes we almost wondered if these firms were conspiring together to tell us the same story! Very often executives from companies in widely different industries echoed each other. For example, on setting high standards one Boeing executive said, "You know that you'll never get 100 percent, but unless you have a very high requirement, you'll never even come close." We heard virtually the same words at Federal Express, Swissair, Xerox, and IBM. Interviewees at Maytag, Deere, and Kodak—three companies in three very different industries—used almost identical phrases when talking about product quality. The list was endless.

### They're Interrelated

Any one of these characteristics, by itself, does not explain why these firms have been successful in implementing a customer-oriented approach to business. Merely being obsessive about customers' needs or demanding high standards of performance or chartering Lear jets won't do the job; it is the total combination that provides a balanced approach and ensures that the firm provides customer satisfaction *at a profit*.

We can visualize the interrelationships between these six characteristics in the form of a five-pointed star (Figure 3.1). It all starts with an internal desire for high performance, a feeling that "the best is barely good enough" for the firm's customers. This creates a pressure to know the customers' needs better than the customers themselves—otherwise how can the firm know what "the best" means? It also helps create and manage customer expectations, for example, "Absolutely, positively overnight," "Nothing *runs* like a Deere," Swissair's image of comfortable, on-time service. Knowing customers' needs and expectations thoroughly enables the various companies to design products and services that maximize customer satisfaction. Finally, they close any gaps between customer expectations and their performance by "putting their money where their mouth is"—chartering Lear jets, issuing "busy day" alerts, providing free loaners—whatever it takes to live up to their commitments.

We have put the sixth characteristic, making customer satisfaction everybody's business, at the center of this star. The reason is that it acts as a mainspring, the driving force that unifies the other five

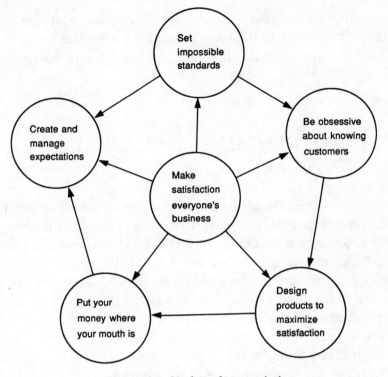

*Figure 3.1 Six key characteristics*

characteristics and provides needed balance. It is this that creates the desire for high standards; when everybody's involved and interested in customer satisfaction, a "let's do it" spirit is created that makes everyone push for higher performance. This spirit also ensures that every department makes knowing the customer its job, and doesn't assume that such knowledge is solely the marketing or sales department's responsibility. This provides direction in creating and managing customer expectations—everybody is vitally interested in what's being promised to the customer and speaks up when they feel that the firm is promising something it can't deliver. It also regulates the debate between the product people—designers, manufacturing, quality control—and finance; you no longer have questions such as, "Oh, it's better, we'll take your word for it, but is it really *that* much better, is it worth all those millions, can you *prove* the benefits?" Finally, it creates the cultural framework that allows everyone within the organization to instinctively *know* when it's right to commit the firm's resources and then go ahead and do it.

## THEY SET THEMSELVES IMPOSSIBLY HIGH STANDARDS

Without exception, each of the companies on our list sets ludicrously high targets for performance and insists that they be achieved. As one executive at Kraft Foodservice explained, "I would like our target service level to be 100 percent, but that really isn't practical . . . [in reality] our target is about 98.7 or 98.8 percent. While that's a lot, it has to be in this business. It's entirely different than a lot of businesses . . . because if you are running a restaurant operation and you ordered cube steak from me on Wednesday and you have that on your menu as a special and it's not there, you don't have any recourse."

Perhaps the most elaborate set of standards is found at Swissair, which distributes surveys to 7000 passengers each quarter and asks them to rate the airline. This is not done in a random fashion. The sample is scientifically selected to get a fair representation of the various routes, types of aircraft, flight schedules, and other variables. The response rate is generally 70 percent or better, meaning that approximately 5000 passengers participate in each quarter. The survey forms go into great detail, covering the airline's performance before, during, and after flight. Customers are asked to rate the airline as excellent, good, fair, or poor. Excellent and good are considered positive ratings and fair and poor are considered negative.

The corporate standard is to have no more than 3 percent negative ratings for overall performance per quarter. This is an astonishing target. What it means is that out of 5000 passengers, no more than 150 should rate Swissair as anything less than good. It is especially impressive when one considers the multitude of problems, some of them beyond human control, that every long-haul airline encounters: missed connections, turbulence, weather delays, equipment failures, and so on.

Swissair has equally rigorous standards for the individual elements of its service. In Zurich, for example, the waiting time at check-in should be no longer than two minutes for at least 90 percent of the airline's first-class passengers. In Basel, the time from the aircraft's arrival on the block to delivery of the last piece of luggage should be no more than 10 minutes. Ground service personnel must achieve positive ratings from at least 90 percent of the passengers for their check-in performance, which includes their attitude and cleanliness, as well as every step of check-in from welcoming passengers to wishing them a good trip.

The airline sends the survey results to the appropriate station managers each quarter. Those whose operations have shown substandard performance must complete within two weeks a written analysis of the problem and a list of steps they have taken to bring performance up to the target level. The airline's general manager explained why the airline takes its standards so seriously: Swissair wants not just to be competitive with other airlines, "but a little bit better in all segments. We have to prove to operators and to individual passengers that it is worthwhile coming through Zurich or flying Swissair on any segment."

Federal Express is another company with impossibly high standards. The company promises that all packages sent via its overnight service to most destinations will be delivered by 10:30 A.M. It offers a money-back guarantee if a package is not delivered on time. In effect, Federal Express' target is 100 percent on-time deliveries.

The difficulty of meeting this standard is especially clear when one realizes the volume and timing of Federal Express' business. The company handles about 750,000 packages each day, many of which are not picked up until the end of the business day. Each package is tracked from the time a courier picks it up until it is delivered. This is done by scanning the package with a minicomputer which then sends the information to Federal Express' central COSMOS system. A package is scanned in the van when it is picked up, at several intermediate points and then, finally, by the courier when it is delivered. Proof of delivery, the recipient's name and the time of delivery are also entered into the computer system. According to Federal Express, "There's only one purpose for that [scanning packages]: to be able to tell the customer what the status is, because there's no tomorrow on this package."

Regardless of weather delays, equipment breakdowns, or other problems, these thousands of packages must be delivered between the start of the business day and 10:30 A.M.—a "window" of two or three hours at most. A missed-delivery rate of even 1 percent in one day means that 7500 packages either went astray or just reached their destination sometime after 10:30 A.M. Federal Express recognizes that it simply can't afford to let that happen. "We know that what we ship is so critical that there are not a lot of second chances. You have to do what you say. You have to do it the first time," explained one executive.

There are several reasons these companies set such unattainable goals. One is that the businesses appear to be driven to do so. They hire people who share that esprit de corps, in the same way that the Marines "look for a few good men." IBM has a reputation for this type of commitment, as demonstrated by the service representative who pulled a pair of roller skates from the trunk of her car when she was caught in a traffic jam and skated on to her customer's assistance. The company culture at businesses such as these seems to demand this all-out drive to succeed.

Another, somewhat intangible, reason is that our winners recognize the satisfaction employees feel when they accomplish the impossible. One might expect workers to be frustrated and demoralized by the rigorous demands. We found that the opposite was true. They are motivated to achieve the best. There's a great deal of pride apparent in the motto of the Seabees: "The impossible we do today. Miracles take a little longer." This feeling was typical among the companies that we interviewed.

A third reason for setting high standards is the fallibility of performance measurements. There is a common tendency for people being asked to rate individuals or businesses to sugarcoat their replies, or at least to put them somewhere in the middle of the range between poor and perfect. Imposing extraordinarily high standards is one way to compensate for this "noise" in the measurement process. More dangerous to business than the mere reticence of consumers, though, is the finding of many studies that most dissatisfied customers don't give the company a hint of their displeasure, but simply switch to a competitor and tell their family and friends about their dissatisfaction. One study found, for example, that an astounding 96 percent of dissatisfied customers never complain to the company—but between 60 and 90 percent of them switch to the competition. Thus every complaint that *is* registered represents dozens more that are not. For every notch that performance standards are raised, a company attracts and retains the loyalty of these dozens of extra customers.

Finally, these companies realize that performance often falls short of expectations. Therefore, in order to deliver merely good results, they must set their sights on impossible goals. For the executives that we interviewed, knowing that they are likely to achieve something less than what they aim for is the most compelling reason that they can give for aiming for the best.

## THEY ARE OBSESSIVE ABOUT KNOWING WHAT THE CUSTOMER WANTS

The winning companies spend enormous amounts of energy and money to find out what the customer wants. They do this because they want to know what their customers want today, expect tomorrow, and are likely to ask for the day after. They really want to "get inside their customers' skins" as it were, they want to know their customers' needs better than customers themselves. This enables them to anticipate these needs in designing their products and services. It also allows them to create and control the expectations customers may have about their performance.

Swissair's extensive quarterly survey, which was described earlier, is only one way the airline finds out what its customers are thinking; it also performs monthly surveys and distributes a short questionnaire to every passenger.

Throughout the year IBM samples at least 5000 customers regarding their needs and concerns. It surveys its sales representatives and systems engineers for problems, concerns, customer reactions every 90 days. Also, it makes sure that senior executives are involved; every IBM senior manager has a number of accounts where he or she is making sales calls, listening to problems, and so forth.

Deere works equally hard, in formal and informal ways, at knowing and tracking its customers. Company executives from all departments—marketing, engineering, manufacturing, service—talk frequently to hundreds of farmers, people at agricultural-engineering schools, and other farming experts. Deere also conducts periodic sales branch interviews, bringing together management, dealers, and customers.

While many of these activities may appear similar to what other firms do, there are important, although intangible, differences:

1. *Top-to-Bottom Involvement.* Knowing the customer is not considered marketing or, worse yet, market research's job alone. Everyone gets involved, from the president downward. Executives at all levels make it their business to learn about customers and their needs.

2. *Cross-Functional Involvement.* These firms make certain that every department participates in learning about the customer. Lis-

ten to IBM chairman John Opel, "No matter what the primary discipline—finance, manufacturing—you have to know and experience the excitement of sales." While they may not make many sales, these executives learn about customer needs firsthand. Swissair makes certain that all executives are familiar with the results of its quarterly surveys. Xerox presents the findings to every engineer and designer and makes certain that they spend time with the customer. Everyone gets involved.

3. *Informal as Well as Formal Contacts.* One of the most interesting (and to the people affected, occasionally frustrating) features was that, to the executives of these firms, the customer was not a statistic. Rather, they valued informal contacts with individual customers; they wanted their knowledge of the buyer to have a human face. They were not comfortable with surveys alone; they wanted to know what *individual* customers—sometimes ones they had called on personally—had to say.

4. *A Degree of Hypersensitivity about Customer Needs.* To some extent we found that "when one of their customers sneezes, the firm catches pneumonia." These firms were extraordinarily sensitive to every nuance in their customers' responses, almost hypersensitive.

These differences have a significant qualitative impact. Top management involvement means that the salesforce and marketing department are pushed to study the customer that much harder; after all, these two areas do not want to be caught in the embarrassing position of finding out that they know less than the president does about customer needs. Cross-functional involvement reduces the need to educate engineering, manufacturing, and other departments about what the customer wants; in many cases, these departments know it almost at the same time as the marketing department does. The informal contacts help keep the focus firmly on individual needs and provides a good mental picture that everyone can share. Few people relate to the "average" or the "80th percentile" customer in the abstract. Finally, the hypersensitivity reinforces the importance of knowing customer needs intimately and provides constant pressure, essential in any large organization, to maintain the intensity of customer focus.

## THEY CREATE AND MANAGE CUSTOMER EXPECTATIONS

How satisfied customers are with a given product or service depends as much on their expectations and on their perceptions of performance, as it does on the actual, measurable quality of the product or service itself. In the words of a Swissair executive:

> The individual feeling of receiving quality (i.e., satisfaction) or not is a ratio of *perception to expectation*. In the perception first there is the performance of the crew in an absolute sense and an effective service method and service material. There is [also] the quality of the product you offer. Then comes sympathy and antipathy: If you don't like somebody, your perception changes. The emotional level of the person having the perception plays a role. And group dynamics: You are influenced by the way your neighbor or other people feel.

> On the expectation side, of course you have to have effective sales promotion; your expectation is influenced by propaganda, by sales promotion. Then you have your own previous experience—"I have flown on Swissair, I know how it is"—so you bring that with you in your expectation. You have information from third persons outside the company who tell you how TWA or Swissair is. Then you have more emotional things like national pride—especially for the Swiss. The Swiss are very critical because they expect a lot from Swissair.

Therefore, to keep customers happy it is essential that companies create the right expectations about their products and services as well as control, as best they can, customers' perceptions about their performance.

The companies we researched create and manage customers' expectations in the following three ways:

1. They control their communications—advertising messages, atmospherics, promises sales personnel make, promotion programs—to ensure that they are not overselling their customers or making promises they could not keep.

2. They choose their intermediaries—dealers, distributors, sales agents—carefully, and manage them closely, to ensure that they are creating the right expectations.

3. They manage performance versus expectations very closely—they prefer to underpromise, then deliver more than they promised, thereby increasing customer satisfaction.

Maytag, for example, knows that customers are willing to pay a premium price for its appliances because "They expect more from Maytag," largely as a result of its advertising. It also knows that its customers will complain vociferously about a problem that they would have accepted from another brand. Maytag creates high expectations but doesn't oversell its product. One executive said: "We put the money behind the product to produce it in such a satisfactory manner that it is, in fact, very dependable, very reliable, and it does what the consumer wants the appliance to do, without falling apart." In other words, the company won't promise quality that it can't provide.

Our winners also make certain that their corporate communications and their salespeople are sending the same message to customers. Thus, Northwestern Mutual, for instance, requires that all local advertising by its agents be cleared through the home office. The company gives its agents the specific language they should use in describing policies to prospective customers, such as emphasizing that dividends are not guaranteed.

These companies also recognize the crucial role that intermediaries play in creating and managing customer expectations:

☐ Northwestern Mutual recruits and trains a superior force of agents: Most are college graduates; 25 percent have won membership in the Million-Dollar Roundtable, compared to an average of 4 percent for the top 20 companies; 35 percent are Chartered Life Underwriters, compared to an average of 6 percent for the top 20; and one-third of the agents have received the National Quality Award. A network such as this offers a strong foundation for customer satisfaction. It creates the right, businesslike image that Northwestern wants to project to its policyowners.

☐ Deere and Caterpillar, both companies with excellent dealer organizations, control the appearance and atmospherics of their dealers very closely. Deere, for example, provides extensive assistance in designing the dealership's layout and arranging in-store displays. It also insists that dealership personnel be dressed in green slacks and yellow shirts, to help portray the friendly but businesslike image Deere wants to present to farmers.

☐ Jaguar's many problems in the 1970s were compounded by an inadequate dealership network. One of the first steps the company took to reverse its fortunes was to trim more than half of its Canadian dealers and many of its dealers in the United States.

The winners also try to deliver more than they have promised. Federal Express promises to have the package to the recipient by 10:30 A.M. the next day; in most cases it is delivered by 9 or 9:30. Similarly, Xerox trains its service representatives to underpromise and overdeliver: When a customer calls with a problem, the service technician schedules a visit at a time he or she is absolutely certain it can be achieved. The technician usually manages to arrive earlier than expected, thereby increasing customer satisfaction. Nor does he or she stop there; Xerox has trained its technicians to follow up with a telephone call a day or so later to find out if everything is still functioning well. This further improves customer satisfaction; it also catches any problems that may not have been fixed correctly the first time without the customer having to call back.

## THEY DESIGN THE PRODUCT TO MAXIMIZE CUSTOMER SATISFACTION

Our winners design their products and services to meet the needs of their most demanding customers. They are not interested in offering an average product that is just good enough for an average customer, or even a slightly better than average product for a slightly more demanding than average customer. They strive for superlatives, even if it means overengineering, or "gold-plating" the product.

Jaguar, for example, knows that its cars are driven in all climates. Consequently, it tests them at widely different locations under extreme conditions, such as Death Valley and northern Canada. Every three months, the company calls in its service directors from the "four extremes in the world": the Middle East, where the climate is the hottest; Canada, where it's coldest; Germany, where drivers are the fastest; and Australia, where drivers are the roughest. Changes recommended by any one of the service directors are included in all cars. As a result, the company said, every Jaguar has a heating system that will handle the Canadian cold, air conditioning that can defeat desert heat, enough speed for the Autobahn, and enough ruggedness for the Australians.

Like Jaguar, Boeing must satisfy a diverse assortment of airline customers. Some airlines are based at high-altitude airports, others at low altitudes; some are in hot and humid locations, others at cold and dry ones; some airlines have long-range flight requirements, others make only short hauls. Boeing goes to great lengths to get assistance from its customers to create flexible aircraft designs that will accommodate the widest range of operating conditions.

Maytag similarly produces the same automatic washers and dryers for private residential use as it does for commercial laundries. The only difference, one Maytag executive said, is that "one's got a coin slot on it and one doesn't." Swissair adheres to its high performance standards at every airport, regardless of the special local problems the airline may encounter. At Bombay airport in India, where Swissair offers one flight a day, the company hired its own baggage-handling service because the airport's service wasn't speedy enough. Federal Express uses a computerized scanning system that helps it pinpoint the location of any package in its network. Not all customers will inquire about the status of a delivery, but those who do ask the question will get an answer within 30 minutes—or their money back.

Why go to such extremes? Why not design for the average user and, if necessary, provide heavy-duty models for the extremes? Our winners design for the most demanding customers for two reasons:

☐ How well the product is designed ultimately determines how much customer satisfaction the company can deliver.

☐ By designing for the extreme user, the company (1) minimizes the number of customers likely to be dissatisfied with the product and (2) accommodates the inevitable growth in the needs of the average user without the need for expensive redesign.


A product or service that has customer satisfaction built in to its design from the very beginning is an invaluable asset; on the other hand, one that is sloppily designed is a continuing drain. Federal Express' Courier Pak™ service was designed for customers who worked late and wanted delivery early—the extremes. Federal Express would pick the package up as late as 7 or 7:30 in the evening and get it there by 10:30, *even if the pickup was on the West Coast and the delivery was on the East Coast*. Contrast this with the Postal Service's Express Mail: You had to get the package to the post office before 5 P.M. and it would be delivered sometime before 3:30 in the afternoon the next day. No wonder Courier Pak™ was a winner from the start.

On the other hand, IBM's "chiclet"-style keyboard for its PCjr™ was a continuous drain on its resources. It probably met the needs of the average or occasional user, but the more demanding users were having none of it. Partly as a result, the company ultimately had to write off the model, causing it to suffer a financial embarrassment as well as to lose face with its customers. IBM should have known better; after all, its Selectric™ keyboard was the standard for comfort and operator convenience.

When the company designs for the extreme user, the 80th or 90th percentile, it minimizes the number of customers that are likely to be dissatisfied with its products—10 or 20 percent as opposed to nearly half when the firm designs with the average customer in mind. AT&T telephones are a good example. Designed to stand up to extreme abuse, such as being dropped from the table by a preoccupied caller or slammed down by an angry teenager, AT&T phones have captured a large share of the market. Initially, customers tried cheaper imports, but once they found that these phones were not as rugged, they quickly switched to the reliable AT&T handset.

Designing for the extreme user also allows the company to accommodate any growth in the needs of the customer without problems. For example, the Maytag washer and dryer that is built to meet the needs of a commercial coin-operated laundry will have no trouble handling the extra loads imposed by a new baby.

A company can derive sustained benefits from designing products to provide maximum satisfaction. It takes a long time for customers to outgrow a reliable, comfortable, and durable design.

For proof, look at products as diverse as the AT&T telephone, the Jeep, the IBM Selectric™ keyboard, and the F4 Phantom jet fighter.


## THEY PUT THEIR MONEY WHERE THEIR MOUTHS ARE

This one characteristic, above all others, separated our winners from the rest. These firms consistently committed resources to meet their commitments to their customers, almost regardless of what it might cost. There were numerous examples of this approach among the companies we researched:

☐ In 1981 Kraft Foodservice went through a slow period and had to cut headquarters staff 45 percent. Even though money was extremely tight, the company invested a major sum in a vehicle scheduling system which, down the road, would prove to be an extremely important tool in improving customer satisfaction. They also decided to increase the salesforce at least 25 percent a year and conducted a major advertising campaign in the trade press about the things Kraft would do for its customers.

☐ A Kodak customer told of buying a Kodak camera in West Germany and using it during his travels through Europe until it failed while he was in London. He brought it to a Kodak office in London and the clerk replaced it on the spot, no questions asked.

☐ Boeing requires that when a customer requests an AOG (aircraft-on-ground) part, the item must be on the shipping dock and ready to go within two hours. If the part isn't in stock, it will be taken from an airplane on the production line in order to meet this deadline.

☐ Maytag faced a shortage of steel when some of its suppliers were shut down for a time in the 1950s. The company could have bought from offshore suppliers. Their steel, however, lacked the zinc coating that Maytag insisted on using to prevent rust. The difference would not have been apparent to customers, since the steel is covered by paint and porcelain. Nonetheless, Fred Maytag II, the company's chief executive officer said that, "we are not going to compromise short-term the quality of our product," one company official remembered. Maytag refused to buy the foreign steel and the company suffered production problems, losing sales and profits, until its regular suppliers were back in business.

Nor were these merely responses to isolated or unexpected problems; rather they are built into our winners' operations. Northwestern Mutual Life Insurance Company calls its customers "policyowners" instead of "policyholders" to reinforce in everyone's mind who's the boss. Beyond that, however, every year its board of directors appoints five policyowners to an examining committee. The committee spends five days (at company expense) with full access to records—and executives—at corporate headquarters in Milwaukee. The committee's job is to scrutinize, question, challenge, and examine the company's operations. Its report on its findings is included in Northwestern Mutual's annual report.

Swissair knows that punctuality is critical, since many of its passengers are connecting to and from other long-range flights. Fuel conservation is also an important issue in controlling expenses. But there's no doubt about which comes first: The company's priorities, listed in its operations manual, are in order of priority, safety, comfort, punctuality, and economy. The manual instructs the captain to use high-speed cruise—a move that significantly increases fuel consumption—when the flight is delayed beyond a certain point. This is total folly in terms of fuel conservation, Swissair says, but essential to passenger satisfaction.

Xerox provides another example of a system that places satisfaction above all else. A few years ago the company planned to introduce a new product in the low-end market. As the deadline for launching the product approached, however, Xerox realized that it had to choose between meeting the deadline with a product that didn't meet its standards for quality, or delaying the introduction until the quality aspect was built in. Xerox chose to delay delivery—a decision that cost the company a considerable amount of money.

These companies go to such extraordinary lengths to provide customer satisfaction for a number of reasons. First, it helps close the inevitable gap between the performance of their products/services and what customers want. Airlines understand that parts fail; what they want is rapid replacement. Consumers similarly understand that, occasionally, new cameras break down; all they want is hassle-free replacement regardless of where they happen to be when the failure occurs. It also avoids potential future problems: By speeding up its planes, Swissair helps minimize complaints about missed connections. Maytag similarly avoided potential future trouble by refusing to accept substandard steel.

Second, it convinces customers that "This company means what it says," that it's not just another advertising campaign. This sets the company apart from its competitors. It also makes the company's claims more believable. Finally, it helps the firm overcome any short-term product problems. Federal Express' slogan, "absolutely, positively overnight," is more believable because people *know* that, if there's a way to get it there, Federal Express will deliver. They don't doubt it or question it; they take it for granted. Deere was able to capture a large chunk of the four-wheel drive tractor market in the mid-1970s despite a product that had significant reliability problems. The reason? Farmers knew—and *believed*—that Deere would fix the problems, regardless of cost (as indeed Deere did). The examples go on and on.

Perhaps even more important, it convinces employees that the company means what it says, that customer satisfaction is not merely a slogan but a central part of the way the firm does business. This has several important benefits. First, it reinforces and strengthens "customer-oriented" behavior. Since actions speak louder than words, a simple thing such as sending a cab to pick up a package has far more impact than all the slogans and speeches. Second, it shows employees how seriously commitments are taken. This enhances their confidence when they promise customers something. Further, it extends beyond the sales organization; the service technician feels comfortable promising that parts will arrive on a certain day, the shipping clerk can predict when a shipment will leave, the finance department can commit to complete the paperwork by a certain date, without worrying if the salesperson will get the details there in time.

The fact that a company means what it says has two important, if intangible, side benefits. Knowing how seriously the firm takes commitments, everybody is less inclined to oversell. When you know that the firm will send a jet to pick up a single package—and that the cost of that jet may be docked against your department—you're much more careful about what you promise, and to whom. This ensures that the firm creates the right expectations, that it doesn't promise what it can't deliver. It also means that employees will go the extra mile to meet commitments within their regular duties. They all know what a missed shipment or a delayed delivery might cost if they make a mistake or overlook something, and they are determined to avoid it.

## THEY MAKE CUSTOMER SATISFACTION EVERYBODY'S BUSINESS

Every employee in these firms is intensely and personally interested in keeping the customer happy. That literally means everyone from the file clerk, baggage handler, or trainee, up to the chairman of the board.

In interview after interview we asked, "What's the secret to your company's success?" Repeatedly the answer came back, "There's no secret you can identify. It's many things, but at the heart of it is dedication to quality throughout the company. . . . We try to get all of our employees involved." Quality, service, reliability, commitment—the words were different, but in each company the sentiments were the same.

This, and this alone, is the key to the winners' success. They get all their employees in every department or function closely involved in the effort to provide superior customer satisfaction. It's as simple—and as complex—as that. Everything else they do— being obsessive about knowing the customer, setting extremely high standards, designing products that maximize customer satisfaction—is aimed solely at achieving this one overriding goal.

There is a compelling logic for fostering this total involvement. If the whole process of designing, producing, and selling is to be geared toward customer satisfaction, then the entire organization must be held responsible for it. In the 1970s Jaguar had a well-designed car but few sales because of poor supplier performance, indifferent morale in manufacturing, and inadequate dealers. The total involvement was missing and customers went elsewhere.

By fostering this total involvement, our winners avoid suboptimization—the "it's not my problem; customer service can deal with it" mentality. In most companies keeping customers happy is the sole responsibility of the salesforce while the other departments pursue their own objectives. This division creates two major problems:

☐ It isolates other departments from direct contact with customers and their needs. This makes it more difficult to design products that satisfy, adapt advertising to create the right expectations, provide sympathetic attention to complaints—in short, change departmental objectives as customers' requirements shift.

☐ In turn, this isolation creates a lack of accountability to the customer, a sense that cutting costs, reducing paperwork, improving profit margins, or other *internal* goals are more important than keeping customers happy. This lack of accountability also fatally biases the "cost versus customer" argument in favor of cost reductions and against investments in customer satisfaction: Most of the managers participating in the debate lack any hands-on involvement with the customer and therefore are less sympathetic to his or her needs. "Objective" facts replace subjective beliefs.

Furthermore, our winners create this total involvement *because* of their concern for profits, not in spite of it. Harvey Lamm, president of Subaru of America, Inc., expressed the common sentiment when he said, "To satisfy the customer, it means that everybody in the company has to understand that the total existence of a company depends upon the customer, so if the customer is not satisfied, he is not going to be a customer tomorrow, and if he is not a customer tomorrow, we don't have a business tomorrow."

In many cases, this attitude was built in by the company's founders. In 1888 Northwestern Mutual Life Insurance Company's executive committee decreed that "Northwestern will not seek to be the biggest, but the best. It will put policyowners first and attempt to provide fair and equal treatment to all policyowners, those who bought insurance many years ago as well as those buying it today." In Maytag's lobby there is a quote from Frederick L. Maytag II, the grandson of the founder, "To be successful, you've got to serve the interests of the shareholders, dealers, customers, and employees." IBM's service attitude dates back to Thomas J. Watson, Sr.'s insistence on keeping the customer happy. The Federal Express motto, "People, Service, Profits," is ingrained in every worker. These traditions encourage employees to go to extreme lengths to help the customer without fear of punishment, even if it costs the company money.

Senior management reinforces the message by its own actions demonstrating that the motto is more than just words, that it is something to be practiced. Top executives at Delta Airlines pitch in and help the baggage handlers at Christmas time. Harvey Lamm reads every customer letter sent to him personally and expects his subordinates to do likewise. The president of Six Flags Corp., Daniel Howells, reads all customer complaints and visits the company's amusement parks unannounced and incognito to see that all guests are satisfied.

Everyone—not just top management, marketing, the salesforce, or customer service—is involved in the drive for customer satisfaction. Northwestern Mutual recently implemented a wholesale reorganization, changing the structure of jobs at its corporate headquarters. Employees who previously stuck to narrow tasks and who had little or no contact with customers—defined as agents as well as policyowners—now deal frequently with both. The changes resulted in increased accountability, improved performance, and greater satisfaction on the part of customer and employee alike. Xerox makes customer satisfaction an important element in the evaluation of employees, even those who might be considered far removed from the customer. For instance, 25 percent of the performance evaluation of the chief engineer of a product is based on customer satisfaction.

# APPENDIX 1
# SURVEY INSTRUMENT

Overall, our interest is in determining the role that customer satisfaction plays in _____ corporate goals, objectives, and long-term strategies. We are particularly interested in your views on the following, across-the-board questions:

1. In your opinion, how important is the role played by customer satisfaction in the overall success of _____?
2. What specific actions and investments has _____ made in pursuit of superior customer satisfaction?
3. What have been the tangible results—qualitative and quantitative—of these investments?

We would also appreciate your thoughts on the following specific areas relating to customer satisfaction. Please provide examples where possible.

## 1. Product

1.1. What is _____ focus in designing products for its major market segments, and how does customer satisfaction enter into the design?
1.2. What elements of product design do you consider crucial in providing customer satisfaction? Why? Some elements of design that can offer customer satisfaction:
   a. Reliability
   b. Serviceability
   c. Performance
1.3. What is the corporate strategy concerning the product cost versus customer satisfaction trade-off in product de-

sign? What is the relative importance of these two attributes in management's eyes? How is the trade-off considered in the elements of product design? How is it implemented?

1.4. How does customer satisfaction enter into your pricing decisions? Examples of conflicts and of trade-offs made would be very helpful.

1.5. To what extent does customer satisfaction affect purchasing/procurement decisions? Any examples?

1.6. What investments has _____ made in manufacturing that relate explicitly to improving customer satisfaction?

1.7. How are trade-offs made between a design that provides potentially greater customer satisfaction at higher manufacturing cost versus one that is easier/cheaper to manufacture but provides lower customer satisfaction?

1.8. To what extent does _____ seek customer ideas and opinions in designing new products? How does this compare with other manufacturers?

1.9. From which customers, and for which areas of product design, do you seek this input?

1.10. What effect has customer input had on product design? Provide overall and specific examples.

## 2. Before and During Sales

2.1. In your experience, to what extent do the "atmospherics"—background, presentation, attire of the sales force, and so forth—contribute to customer satisfaction? How does _____ control these variables?

2.2. How does your communication program—advertising,

promotions, brochures, and so forth—affect customer satisfaction? What is your strategy in this area?

2.3. How do you control sales attitudes and practices? How does this affect customer satisfaction?

### 3. After Sales

3.1. What after-sales services do you provide? What is their relative importance in customer satisfaction? Examples: warranties, emergency 800 numbers, and so forth.

3.2. What variables does _____ use to measure service quality? In your opinion, how do these variables relate to customer satisfaction?

3.3. How does _____ obtain customer feedback relating to service satisfaction, both in terms of the media used for the feedback (letters, telephones, toll-free or 800 numbers, surveys, etc.) and the areas covered (quality, reliability, performance, dealer relations, etc.)?

3.4. How aggressively does _____ solicit customer feedback?

3.5. What standards or goals, such as response time or resolution time, have you established for the disposition of customer problems and complaints?

3.6. How well do you meet those standards? Please give examples of notable successes or problems.

3.7. What are the most commonly mentioned problem areas that affect customer satisfaction? How does _____ compare in this respect against other leading competitors?

3.8. How does _____ handle customer complaints and requests for exchanges or refunds?

### 4. Corporate Attitudes and Values

4.1. What is the role of customer satisfaction in _____ corporate mission and strategic plans? What is its relative importance compared to other corporate goals?

4.2. What are the incentives, controls, design objectives, and so forth, that are used to reinforce the importance of customer satisfaction?

4.3. For what purposes does _____ pursue or acquire new technology? Give examples.

4.4. What have been the purposes of recent major capital investments by _____?

# 4

## *The Four Fundamentals of Customer Satisfaction*

A variety of factors affect customer satisfaction. Quality, for instance, is a key influence; surveys of consumer and industrial buyers regularly show quality at the top of their concerns. Communications such as advertisements, promotions, and in-store atmospherics play an important role by creating expectations that may or may not be met, resulting in either satisfaction or dissatisfaction. For many products after-sales support such as warranties, service, parts availability, and training vitally affect customer satisfaction. Also, corporate culture and values have a powerful influence, as we have already seen in the case of our winners.

Any one of these variables, by itself, does not completely determine customer satisfaction. A high-quality product with good, appealing design will not guarantee happy customers, as Fiat's and Olivetti's experiences in the United States demonstrate. Despite reliable products, good software, and many dedicated dealers, Texas Instruments has consistently ranked last among the major minicomputer manufacturers. The reason: a corporate culture that was product- and cost-oriented and disdained marketing. Frank Borman changed the culture of Eastern Airlines radically, and tried to make it customer-focused, yet his efforts were doomed by Eastern's route structure and fleet mix (its product) and its poor image in the marketplace (expectations).

These and other similar examples made it clear that we needed a framework to help us organize the data we had collected, analyze the relative importance of each variable, study the interrelationships among the variables, and measure their cumulative impact on customer satisfaction. We had two additional requirements: (1) we wanted a framework that would be flexible enough to cover a wide range of products, services, and industries; and (2) we wanted a framework that would serve as a diagnostic tool.

## THE FOUR FUNDAMENTALS

Our research clearly defines four distinct factors: product-related variables, sales activity-related variables, after-sales variables and culture-related variables. The product factor includes such things as the basic design of the product, how familiar designers are with customer needs, what incentives drive the designers, manufacturing, and quality control. Underlying the sales activity factor are variables such as what messages the company sends out in its advertising and promotion programs, how it chooses and monitors its salesforce/intermediaries, and the attitudes they project to the customer. After-sales includes such things as warranties, parts and service, feedback, complaint handling, and overall responsiveness to a customer with a problem. Culture covers the intrinsic values and beliefs of the firm as well as the tangible and intangible symbols and systems it uses to instill these values into its employees at all levels. The overall framework is shown in Figure 4.1.

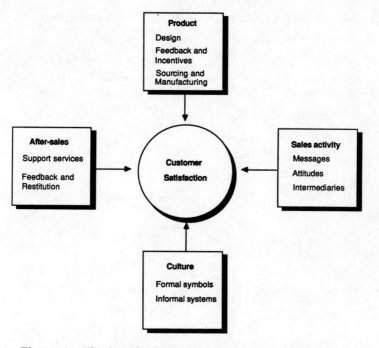

*Figure 4.1 The four fundamentals of customer satisfaction*

In the remainder of this chapter we will discuss the components of each of these four factors in detail. We will then describe how our framework can be used as a diagnostic tool to identify potential areas. Finally, with the help of this framework, we will analyze how long it will take a firm to significantly improve customer satisfaction with its products or services.

## PRODUCT

Three key variables determine how the product or service itself affects customer satisfaction: the basic design of the product; the care with which inputs are chosen, or sourcing decisions; and the actual production process itself. Design can be broken down further into the messages the basic design sends to the customer,

TABLE 4.1   Components of the Four Fundamentals

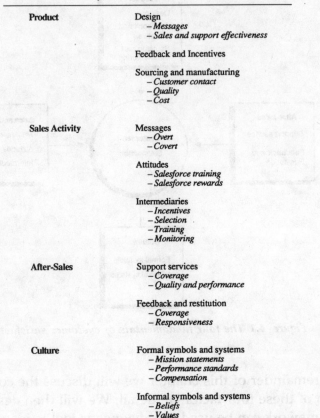

| Product | Design |
|---|---|
|  | – Messages |
|  | – Sales and support effectiveness |
|  |  |
|  | Feedback and Incentives |
|  |  |
|  | Sourcing and manufacturing |
|  | – Customer contact |
|  | – Quality |
|  | – Cost |
| Sales Activity | Messages |
|  | – Overt |
|  | – Covert |
|  |  |
|  | Attitudes |
|  | – Salesforce training |
|  | – Salesforce rewards |
|  |  |
|  | Intermediaries |
|  | – Incentives |
|  | – Selection |
|  | – Training |
|  | – Monitoring |
| After-Sales | Support services |
|  | – Coverage |
|  | – Quality and performance |
|  |  |
|  | Feedback and restitution |
|  | – Coverage |
|  | – Responsiveness |
| Culture | Formal symbols and systems |
|  | – Mission statements |
|  | – Performance standards |
|  | – Compensation |
|  |  |
|  | Informal symbols and systems |
|  | – Beliefs |
|  | – Values |

how the basic design affects sales-and-support effectiveness, how much feedback designers obtain from the customer and to what extent the designers' incentives include customer satisfaction (See Table 4.1).

## Basic Design

This is an obvious, often-overlooked, yet vital determinant of customer satisfaction. People will put up with a lot in terms of poor sales efforts and ragged support for a surprisingly long time if the underlying design is clearly superior. However, superior sales or support cannot carry a poor design for long. The Jaguar XJ-6 Sedan, the Leica M-rangefinder camera, and the Apple II computer are examples of products whose fundamental designs have carried them on far longer than anybody would have predicted through the corporate equivalent of the perils of Pauline: neglect, abuse, shoddy quality, poor dealers, erratic pricing policies, and so forth. The XJ-6 Sedan was designed in 1968 by Sir William Lyons, underwent three modifications, was almost made extinct by atrocious manufacturing quality in the late 1970s, and survived to spark Jaguar's turnaround in the early 1980s. The basic Leica M-series 35-mm rangefinder camera was introduced in the mid-1950s. Made obsolete by the single-lens-reflex Nikons in the 1960s, it was virtually abandoned by the parent company through a combination of spotty dealer representation and extremely high prices. It has survived because of its inherent appeal to demanding professionals and amateurs. On the time scale used by microcomputer makers, the Apple II, introduced in 1978, is prehistoric: only an 8-bit computer with slow disk drives and a funny, small screen. Two generations later, the Apple II still provides a large portion of Apple's revenues and profits, surviving two years of neglect while its glamorous sibling, the Macintosh, took center stage.

Conversely, superb support, lavish advertising, and aggressive marketing didn't help Ford sell the Edsel in 1959, Deere sell bicycles in the 1970s, or IBM sell minicomputers against Digital Equipment. Customers saw through the protective layers and decided they didn't like what they were getting.

### How Product Design Affects Customer Satisfaction

There are two principal ways in which the basic design of a product affects customer satisfaction. First, it provides tangible evidence to the customer regarding the firm's basic values. Second, it can place limits on the firm's maneuverability in terms of sales and support.

*Every Design Sends "Messages" to the Customer.* These mostly subliminal messages are sent to the customer, regarding the following questions:

1. "How does the firm view me: as a vital ingredient to its success or as a necessary evil?" This is the outward manifestation of the basic trade-off, cost versus customer. Subliminally, customers make up their own minds, sometimes on the basis of superficial evidence, as to the firm's real focus. Further, if this subliminal message conflicts with others, such as advertising and sales presentations, customers are still likely to be influenced by the basic design.

2. "What compromises has the firm made?" Implicit in this is the unspoken second half: ". . . and who's getting the benefit?" For years, my colleagues and I avoided Eastern Airlines, in part because of a subjective feeling that Eastern would do anything to avoid serving a meal in-flight. This included departures scheduled at 7:02 P.M., thereby missing the mandatory dinner hour by two minutes; apparently pointless intermediate stops to break up a longer flight—anything! Similarly, Express Mail requires the user to make a trip to the post office and wait until 3 P.M. the next day for delivery, unless he or she is willing to pay an extra charge. These requirements certainly help the Postal Service; it can cut costs and use regular mail delivery personnel. But users perceive the savings as coming at the customer's expense. Fundamentally, the buyer wants to know if the firm has "skinned" the product— taken value out of it in terms of missing features and inconvenient design compromises—to boost the firm's profitability.

3. "How effectively will the product meet my needs?" The real issue here is, "Who has to do the compromising—the company or the customer—where, and why?" Will the design stretch to meet my needs or do I have to shrink to fit into the product design? European shirts come with fixed sleeve lengths; buy a shirt with a

16-inch (42 cm) collar, and the sleeves will be between 33 and 34 inches long. If you wear a 35-inch sleeve, you're out of luck; you'd better figure on shrinking to fit into the standard size.

4. "Will it merely satisfy my needs, or will I be happy?" This is the end result of an often entirely subconscious decision process. At the margin, buyers opt for happiness, not just satisfaction—as soon as they have an affordable choice. They will do this even if they have to pay a premium. Obviously, the design of the product plays a crucial role. Most Detroit compacts perform about as well as comparable Japanese cars, and often cost less. Then why do consumers pay a premium to buy a Honda? Because it "fits" better. Everything is just so (e.g., the driver doesn't have to lean forward to turn on the radio; it's right there, at his or her fingertips).

***Product Design Can Limit Sales-and-Support Effectiveness.*** A poor design can drastically hamstring the firm's ability to keep the customer happy during and after the sale. Timex's rugged, "disposable" design made it possible to persuade customers to buy the watch from pharmacies and supermarkets, not just jewelers, while the IBM PCjr's™ "chiclet" keyboard, incompatible storage media, and other design problems turned it into an albatross. Product design can affect sales- and support-related variables in a number of ways:

1. *It Can Affect Sales Personnel Attitudes and Training.* A strong, successful design increases sales confidence and makes it easier to train salespeople (and ultimately the user) in the product, while a poor design imposes an additional burden, making the sales organization react defensively. Apple's Macintosh-based desktop publishing system is easy to use, well-integrated, and meets most business-users' needs. No wonder it is beating out other systems which are not easy to use and are more expensive.

2. *It Can Constrain Advertising and Promotion Efforts.* If the design makes too many compromises with customer requirements, it inevitably affects the advertising and promotion plans, since the

firm must spend valuable time defending its choices. Travel advertising for "bargains" abounds in restrictions (e.g., certain days only, subject to availability, based on double occupancy, taxes not included, etc.).

3. *It May Limit the Channel Choices.* Xerox's service-intensive designs may have prevented it from using office equipment dealers to cater to the low-end market, thereby creating an opening for Japanese entrants. Canon's disposable cartridge, on the other hand, opened up more channels such as discount stores, mass merchandisers, and mail order.

4. *It Can Increase User Complaints and Problems.* The poor reliability of the Apple III computer probably exacerbated users' disenchantment with a basic design that was considered inadequate. Similarly, IBM suffered a blow to its credibility when its early PC-AT models had serious problems with the hard disk drive.

5. *It Can Add Significantly to the Cost of Providing Support Services.* Designs that are difficult to service, that operators find difficult to use, that have high failure rates—these and other problems can add significantly to the cost of providing adequate levels of support to the customer. In the 1970s Olivetti lost a lot of money in the North American office equipment market for precisely this reason.

### Feedback and Incentives

The degree to which a firm's designs improve customer satisfaction is determined by several factors, such as explicit customer satisfaction goals and standards, how the firm obtains customer comments about innovations, the underlying design philosophy, the priority assigned to ease of product use, and how enhancements to the product are made. We can understand the impact of these variables by (1) studying how the firm's designers obtain feedback from the marketplace and (2) analyzing the designers' formal and informal incentives. We have found that the more closely and directly the designer listens to customer needs and concerns, the more likely that the end product will provide high degrees of customer satisfaction. How much attention the designer pays to the customer, in turn, is largely a function of the rewards and incentives provided by the company.

## Sourcing and Manufacturing

Although the basic design plays a major role in affecting customer satisfaction, the quality of the raw materials used as well as the manufacturing processes and controls also contribute. Many companies that provide high levels of customer satisfaction insist on controlling a high percentage of their raw materials and manufacturing processes. Maytag buys raw rubber and manufactures its own seals and gaskets, in part to ensure that these critical components meet its high standards of durability. Rolls Royce buys its hides and veneers from exclusive sources and keeps selections in stock for all the cars it builds, to ensure that the Rolls owner can obtain a matching replacement. McDonald's went so far as to have a new variety of potato developed to meet its exacting requirements for its french fries. Sears monitors its suppliers closely for adherence to quality. At the other extreme, many of Jaguar's (and the British automotive industry's) quality problems were caused by the poor quality of the parts and assemblies provided by its major suppliers. IBM had to relearn the lesson when it ran into reliability problems on its PC-AT; the culprit was the supplier of the hard disk drive.

To determine the specific relationship that sourcing and manufacturing has with customer satisfaction, we must know the degree to which customer problems are related to these two functions, the relative sensitivity of customer satisfaction measures to changes in manufacturing and purchasing practices, and the implications for the firm's overall cost position and business strategy. In some cases, changes in material inputs or manufacturing processes may be key to improving customer satisfaction, while in others the firm may not have much flexibility in these areas and alternative approaches may have to be used.

## SALES ACTIVITY

Three key factors affect customer satisfaction in this area: messages, attitudes, and intermediaries. *Messages* focus on the variables that condition customer attitudes and expectations before and during the sale. *Attitudes* deal with the sales experience itself, while *intermediaries* refer to the channels used to complete the sale. (See Table 4.1.)

By the time customers are ready to purchase a particular service or product, they have already formed their own ideas about their needs, the benefits a specific product will offer, and the degree of performance and satisfaction that they would like to receive. How happy the customer is with the product will therefore depend on the following:

*How the Presale Phase Was Managed.* Which expectations were created, how were they created, and what attitudes were reinforced or modified?

*How the Customer Was Treated During the Sales Phase.* How well was the salesperson trained in the product's or service's features and applications, what were the sales attitudes and communications during the purchase, what was the focus of sales efforts, and what promises were made and how well were they kept?

*How Well the Channel or Intermediary Was Controlled.* Which intermediaries or channels were used, how were specific members selected, what were the depth and focus of training efforts, how and to what extent were intermediaries controlled, and what incentives were they given?

All of these factors determine which of the customer's attitudes are altered or reinforced, which product is purchased, and how much postpurchase dissatisfaction is likely. If customers buy a product that meets their needs adequately and is a good "fit," there will probably be very few complaints after the sale. However, if customers' expectations were unrealistic and were not modified during the sale, or if the channel created unrealistic expectations during the sale, or if the product was sold on the basis of a "force-fit" (i.e., the product was the right price but it didn't meet the customers' basic requirements) then many complaints can be expected.

### Messages

Customers' attitudes and expectations are affected before the sale by advertising, promotional flyers and offers, product literature, the experiences of other users and purchasers, and, of course, any prior experiences with the company and its products. These attitudes are affected during the sale by price quotations and tactics, product literature, the ease with which the customer can try the product, information about the need for and availability of after-sales support, and the overall atmospherics of the location in which the transaction takes place. We can divide these influencers into *overt* messages—those that the firm creates explicitly— and *covert* messages—subconscious signals sent to the customer, whether intended or not.

*Overt* messages include advertising, promotion, sales literature, special offers and mailings. *Covert* messages include channel atmospherics—decor, salesperson's attire, sales location, store layout, product arrangement, and the overall impression created. The combination of these messages creates a certain set of attitudes about the firm, its products, and the type and degree of satisfaction that customers can expect. For example, all of IBM's overt and covert messages stress the themes of safety and security. Its advertisements rarely focus on specific features or performance comparisons, its sales personnel are always dressed conservatively, the firm rarely, if ever, advertises discounts (and *never* special deals), and the overall theme is very "buttoned down" and businesslike. Consequently, purchasers of IBM equipment rarely complain about the lack of leading-edge technologies and applications or grouse about missing out on special deals or being oversold by a salesperson. In fact, according to Buck Rodgers, IBM's former senior vice president of marketing, IBM has a strongly ingrained principle of not overselling. Violate it, and you are "subject to the most severe disciplinary action." What IBM has done with these messages is very simple:

☐ It has worked hard to create the "right" set of expectations about its products and services—expectations that the company can meet and even exceed.

☐ It has effectively screened out "excessive" or "wrong" expectations, even at the risk of losing customers—such as users wanting the latest solutions and technology.

☐ It has *"pre*sold" customers that IBM's approach is to work with them to solve their problems—thus customers don't expect IBM to sell them a piece of computer equipment; they expect a solution.

☐ It hasn't created misleading impressions about price, but rather has conditioned the customer, subconsciously, to concentrate on security and value.

### Attitudes

Everyone who comes in contact with the customer projects attitudes that affect the customer—the representative calling on the telephone, the receptionist at the door, the service technician making a call to fix other machines on the customer's premises, and the salesperson who actually gets the order. Consciously or subconsciously, the buyer is always evaluating the firm's approach to doing business, how it deals with other customers, and how it is likely to treat him or her.

*Actions.* Attitudes are reflected in actions; the behavior of the various people with whom the customer comes in contact has an impression on the customer's level of satisfaction. This includes:

The overall courtesy of personnel in dealing with inquiries and problems, giving information, or providing services, as well as how the firm deals with other customers;

Their sales knowledge, that is, product knowledge, information about applications, and awareness of the positioning of the product in relation to competitors; and

Their sales focus, that is, whether they concentrate on identifying and meeting their customers' needs or are merely interested in pushing any product, however unsuitable, that will create a sale and put money in their pockets.

Companies attempt to mold the actions/behavior of their employees through *training* and *rewards*.

*Training.* Companies spend large sums of money on product training, but relatively little on customer or industry knowledge, applications training, or learning about the relative advantages and disadvantages of its products versus those of its competitors in different operating situations. These aspects of training, however, often have a significant effect on customer satisfaction. They can help reinforce positive impressions about the firm's products and services while correcting any misconceptions about prices, relative merits as compared with competitors' products, and wrong or incorrect applications. For example, a major source of information for many small- and medium-sized firms buying office equipment such as copiers, PCs, and printers is their service technician, particularly if he or she is associated with a piece of machinery that is functioning satisfactorily. Often, customers accept the advice of these technicians without question. The customers believe the technicians should be knowledgeable, since they see so many different types of equipment, and objective since they're not trying to sell anything. Rarely does a firm spend money on formalizing this information to learn about its customers' concerns or to ensure that its technicians (1) provide its customers with up-to-date evaluations and (2) do not propagate misconceptions.

One of the first things that Century 21 Real Estate Corporation did when it first began was to change the attitudes and sales focus of its franchisees through a training program. This training program was designed to transform the franchisees' emphasis from what had been the traditional commission-centered approach to one that said, "If we take care of the customer by serving his or her needs, the money will come." Bruce Oseland, a senior vice president at Century 21, gave a personal example of the difference this can make: "I worked with three real estate agents (while looking for a house) until I found someone who gave a damn about anything except a house and four walls. The first one I dealt with said, 'We've got a two-bedroom over here and a three-bedroom over here and—what was your name? Bruce. Right, Bruce. . . . ' The second one didn't do any homework and we're out looking around at a map trying to find locations because he heard this house was for sale. . . . Finally, the third one sat down with my wife and I and he talked about our son and where we lived before and what we were looking for, where we worked and all of this, and *then*, after an hour and a half, said, 'By the way, how much money do you make? I need that for . . . ' and then he started going into what I could qualify for, and we left. We never looked at a piece of property. All the others slammed us in the back of their four-door car and got us out there and tried to sell us a house. He identified our needs, he established rapport with us, and the next time we came back, he's got a little folder like this, and inside there's houses. . . . We loved the guy and we bought a house from him. And that's the difference."

*Rewards.* The structure of a firm's reward system determines how various personnel actually behave. In turn, this affects customers' perceptions and influences their satisfaction levels. At IBM, for instance, the reward system encourages long-term participation with the customer and close teamwork. Thus IBM sales personnel, while just as motivated to meet quotas as their counterparts are at other firms, also have to keep the long-term objectives of the company in mind. For example: Returns or nonrenewals of leases are credited against the salesperson handling the account, regardless of who sold the item. Thus every salesperson has an incentive to ensure that the customer is happy with the performance of all IBM equipment and services, and not to concentrate merely on new sales. In evaluating the reward structure, it is essential to include both the formal rewards as well as the informal procedures and policies determining who receives the rewards, as these send strong messages to the rest of the organization about management's true intentions. Thus although the explicit reward system may emphasize account development and customer satisfaction, if the individuals promoted are consistently the big producers, the rest of the salesforce gets the clear message, "Worry more about short-term sales than about long-term, account-building activities." They behave accordingly and the firm's customer relations suffer.

### Intermediaries

In many industries the product is sold through an intermediary such as a dealer, manufacturer's representative, supermarket, corner grocery, or retailer who is not directly controlled by the firm. The behavior of these intermediaries has an important bearing on overall customer satisfaction. In many cases, customers' attitudes toward these intermediaries strongly influence their feelings about the parent firm and its products. Thus the selection of intermediaries, the training they receive, and how they're measured and controlled determines how happy customers will be

with the firm's products. Both Deere and Caterpillar place considerable emphasis in all three areas, with the result that their dealer
networks are major corporate strengths. The local Deere dealer is
usually held in high regard by his or her peers: Often, he or she
sits on the board of the local bank, is active in civic affairs, and is
usually a community leader of some stature. This has definite
benefits for Deere in that the dealer's reputation for honesty and
fair dealing reinforces Deere's image. At times this is extremely
useful, as was the case when Deere introduced its 8430 and 8630
series of four-wheel-drive tractors in the mid-1970s. Because of
teething problems, the early models spent a lot of time in the service shop for repairs. However, the local dealers' strong reputation helped the firm weather the crisis. The dealers helped Deere
get the breathing space it needed to introduce modifications that
solved the initial problems. Thus, from a slow start, the company
was able to capture a major share of the market. On the other
hand, with some exceptions, automotive dealers are often held in
low regard by consumers and this rubs off on the manufacturers
themselves.

## AFTER SALES

Traditionally, most firms' activities related to keeping customers
happy began after the sale, with the customer service desk or the
complaint department. Today, ensuring customer satisfaction after the sale is a major concern for nearly all manufacturers. After-
sales support activities have expanded to include toll-free hotlines, information and advisory services, recall notices, and
consumer alerts, along with such necessities as after-sales repair
and maintenance services, repair parts depots, regular and extended warranties, operator training assistance, extended training for customer personnel, systems to handle modifications and
changes, and so forth.

For industrial equipment and consumer durables such as washers, dryers, and kitchen appliances, these support services are essential if the customer is to consider the company during the purchase decision. Therefore it is no surprise that such companies offer extensive after-sales support services. For packaged goods and services, the need for such services and their relationship to customer satisfaction has been recognized only recently. One of the pioneers in this area was Proctor & Gamble, which prints a toll-free number on all its product labels. In the first year that they did this, the company received more than 250,000 phone calls from customers, providing it with considerable feedback and insight into customers' needs and concerns. General Mills has a similar hotline for its products, dispensing recipes and cooking advice. Federal Express has installed a tracking system with which the company can locate a customer's package rapidly at any stage in its network. Such services appear to be enhancements that these companies are making to their basic product offerings to increase customer satisfaction. They also help the firms monitor customers' concerns. For example, the Proctor & Gamble hotline received calls regarding rumors, based on the company's corporate symbol, of "satanic" influences within the company. Such after-sales services also provide assistance in meeting crises head-on, such as the toxic shock attributed to Rely tampons.

We can categorize the various elements of after-sales support into those relating to specific *support services*, such as warranties, parts and service, user assistance, and training, and those related to *feedback and restitution*, namely complaint handling, dispute resolution, refunds and refund policies, and so forth. (See Table 4.1.)

☐ *Support Services.* Both the range of services offered to the customer and the underlying corporate policies and attitudes have a definite impact on customer satisfaction. Apple Computer's policies regarding upgrades to its products have not always been consistent, leaving an impression with major market segments that its pricing is too high and that the firm doesn't fully recognize the extent of the burden placed on early purchasers of its products and software.

Tandy, on the other hand, provides software upgrades to its registered owners free or at minimal charge. Whirlpool and Maytag maintain an inventory of parts for nearly every model of their machines ever made, including parts for appliances that have been discontinued for 30 years or more. Caterpillar guarantees its customers that they will receive a part within 48 hours, anywhere in the world, or else they get it for free. These and other companies with strong after-sales support reputations have a host of corporate legends detailing how these promises were kept, almost regardless of cost.

☐ *Feedback and Restitution.* This covers specific activities, such as complaint handling, returns, and dispute resolution, as well as how management views these activities' contribution to keeping the customer happy. Some companies have virtually made their national reputation on the basis of their policies in this area. L.L. Bean, a mail-order firm based in Maine, has long been famous for its "no-questions-asked" return policy. For more than 50 years, the firm has told its customers that "no reason needed, no excuse required, no abuse of the article too strong to justify refusing a refund." Although the costs of this return policy are enormous—between 5 and 6 percent of sales—the benefits are obvious: Every page of the L.L. Bean catalog generates on the average $1 million in sales and customer loyalty is extremely strong.

After-sales support is a litmus test of a firm's intentions toward its customers. In effect, the customer judges the company by its willingness to stand behind its products and to provide satisfaction to even the most unreasonable buyer. Handled well, these activities help strengthen the company's franchise with the buyers of its products. For example, Johnson & Johnson's rapid, decisive, and courageous actions in the wake of the Tylenol crisis helped the

firm regain its leading position in the analgesic market; the poi-
sonings are merely an unpleasant memory to most consumers.

## CORPORATE VALUES

Corporate values—an organization's beliefs, norms, thoughts,
and strategies, its overall culture or design for living and competing—are the major drivers behind product, sales activity, and after-sales related variables. If the firm truly believes in the need for
maximizing customer satisfaction to ensure long-term success,
then the product, sales activity, and after-sales elements will be
synchronized, working together to deliver what the organization
wants. On the other hand, if management is merely paying lip
service to customer satisfaction—if instead of being a basic tenet
of the firm, customer satisfaction is merely a fad—the organization cannot deceive its employees or its customers.

Customer satisfaction is the key to IBM's philosophy. Employees
know that they can change or postpone a meeting with the chairman of the board in order to meet with a customer. They also believe that they have the resources, and the responsibility, to move
heaven and earth to find a part or keep a customer working.
These beliefs are strengthened by the "living memory" of the
organization—the stories told by IBM employees and customers
of specific instances wherein the firm performed miracles. Deere's
entire strategy can be summarized in its slogan, "Nothing runs
like a Deere."© Everything and everyone—from design to testing
to manufacturing to sales and right on through the dealer network—are oriented to keeping the customer's machine up and
running. During the harvest season, Deere's shipping docks,
parts personnel, and dealership services departments are open
practically around the clock to keep farmers' combines operating,
assuring them that Deere will do its best to make certain a year's
hard work isn't lost in a single rain or hailstorm. At Xerox, cus-

tomer satisfaction is again becoming a major driver, with all functions participating. For example, on any given product, the chief designer's compensation is intimately tied to how well customers like the product in the field.

Conversely, customers' and employees' memories of past performances hampered Eastern Airlines' efforts to improve its poor reputation for service. Both groups kept asking themselves if the stress on customer satisfaction was merely a temporary phenomenon (the "fad of the month") and wondering when the company's true feelings will emerge. The health-care industry is similarly hampered by a long tradition of benign neglect of the patient. For many customers, this reputation is reinforced at nearly every encounter with a physician. Jaguar provides a revealing example of how culture can both help and hinder a firm's ability to maximize customer satisfaction. In the 1970s, as a subsidiary of British Leyland, the firm's culture almost ignored the customer, with the result that by 1980, Jaguar's U.S. sales—which represented the major portion of its output—had dwindled to 3000 cars per year. A new management team was able to turn the company around dramatically, in large part because employees, dealers, and prospective owners were convinced that the firm really meant what it said about standing behind its cars, improving its reliability record, and doing everything it could to keep the customer happy.

There are two components to cultural values: the *formal* ones espoused by the firm and the *informal* ones that are implicit in its actions. Formal values are those outlined in the company's mission statements and detailed in goals, action plans, policies and procedures, and other explicit control systems. The informal values of the firm are determined over time and, in the long run, are the true measure of the firm's intentions. These informal values are determined by such factors as the degree to which various levels of management are involved, quality of management (especially senior management) involvement, the folklore of the company—the anecdotes, legends, and so on that determine new employees' attitudes and values—and the degree of consistency in implementation. Although the *styles* of individual firms vary considerably—some are almost evangelical in their fervor to be customer-oriented, while others are more understated and structured in their approach—in all cases both the formal and the informal cultural values are consistent in their commitment to customer satisfaction.

## APPLYING THE FRAMEWORK

When a company starts out, it can change any of the four fundamental factors of customer satisfaction it pleases. However, as time goes on the firm will find that its ability to change direction is restricted, either by what it has or has not done in the past or by industry structure and competition, for example, standard or normal practices within the industry, what other firms offer as a promotion or on a regular basis, what customers have come to expect as a minimal level of performance, and so on. As a start-up company, People Express had a clean slate on which to define its approach to customer satisfaction. It could and did charge for such standard things as checked baggage and in-flight food and beverages without necessarily affecting customer satisfaction. On the other hand, Acker, chairman and CEO at Pan Am, was restricted by existing route structure, fleet composition, union contracts, service standards, training procedures, and preexisting image. Thus it took far longer to make significant changes in the level of customer satisfaction delivered.

We can use this framework for diagnosing problems and developing a plan for improving customer satisfaction. The framework provides a diagnostic tool to identify what is preventing the company from providing superior customer satisfaction. Once the major problems have been located we can estimate what it would take (in time and money) to correct them and what alternatives are available.

## Diagnosing the Problem

With the help of the variables that make up each of the four factors, we can create a diagnostic procedure for an individual company as follows:

STEP 1. First we determine how the industry as a whole rates on customer satisfaction. Some industries such as major appliances have a much higher level of overall customer satisfaction than others like automobiles.

STEP 2. We identify the winners within the industry and then evaluate their performance in terms of the four fundamentals.

STEP 3. Based on the results of the first two steps, we create benchmarks against which our firm's performance can be measured.

STEP 4. We now measure the performance of our company. This process will be lengthy, requiring extensive interviews and analyses of existing policies, procedures, systems, incentives, and so forth.

STEP 5. We validate the results of the diagnostic by comparing our performance against the winners in our industry.

This diagnostic procedure will identify key problem areas and help pinpoint likely causes. Based on the results we can develop a plan for making necessary changes.

A diagnostic tool such as this also provides insight into the seriousness of the problem and the length of time it will take to significantly improve customer satisfaction. If the problems are confined to areas such as sales messages or in-field service performance or poor complaint handling, then changes can be made quickly and relatively inexpensively. On the other hand, if the company is performing poorly in terms of two or more of these factors, it is a sign that the problems are very widespread and improvements will be slow in coming and will require substantial investments of time and money.

In general, problems relating to sales activity and after-sales support are easier to correct, while those having their roots in poor design or a cost-oriented customer culture are more difficult.

☐ *Product.* Design-related problems are very difficult to cure in the case of consumer durables and industrial equipment, especially if they require major redesign or reengineering to improve user-friendliness, increase reliability, or add features and functions. Making such changes in services and packaged goods is somewhat easier. Quality problems that originate in manufacturing take longer to solve, as compared with those due to poor sourcing.

☐ *Sales Activity.* Messages and atmospherics are the easiest to change while salesforce/intermediary attitudes and incentives are much harder. Advertising can be rewritten, promotions can be redesigned, and stores and displays can be redecorated. But shifting sales focus away from commissions or production and toward meeting customers' needs requires extensive training, changes in how sales personnel are compensated, and sometimes even major management changes to prevent the old guard from sabotaging efforts to change. Similarly, changing the attitudes of dealers and distributors takes time for retraining, for refocusing, and sometimes for replacement.

☐ *After Sales.* Improving service support performance is relatively easy. Usually it requires nothing more than additional people, greater investments in parts and facilities and a greater emphasis on prompt delivery. However, if the basic design is faulty or has low reliability or is being sold for the wrong applications (causing greater failures), then throwing more money at the field sales organization will merely act as a BandAid.

☐ *Culture.* Of the four factors, this is the most difficult and the most time consuming to change. It is also the most crucial; if the culture does not support a customer-focused attitude then all investments in changing product designs, sales incentives, intermediaries' attitudes, after-sales support, and so forth will be fruitless. Inevitably, once the initial flush of enthusiasm has worn off, the old cost orientation will reassert itself and, sooner rather than later, the company will find itself back where it started.

These differences help explain why Jaguar was able to turn itself around so rapidly while General Motors is finding it extremely difficult to improve customer satisfaction. Jaguar's basic designs were sound; its quality control problems were primarily due to poor sourcing. The small size of the firm coupled with its desperate financial conditions ensured that a new, customer-oriented chief executive, John Egan, would be able to turn management attitudes around quickly. Once the supply problems were solved and manufacturing quality improved, it was a relatively easy task to change sales attitudes, atmospherics, and incentives, and improve after-sales support.

General Motors, on the other hand, has many different designs, produced in much higher volumes and requiring mammoth investments. Its sales and dealer attitudes have been conditioned over three decades to be volume- and cost-oriented, not customer focused. Changing customer expectations through messages and atmospherics will be expensive and will take longer due to the large number of customers and the difficulty of overcoming a long legacy of high-handed, nonresponsive treatment. Improving after-sales support will also be difficult because of the many other intermediaries such as muffler shops, tune-up centers, and mass merchandisers who cannot be controlled by GM but who affect the quality of service delivered. In addition, GM's insular and inbred corporate culture virtually ensures that change, when and if it occurs, will happen at a glacial pace.

Each of these factors: product, sales activity, after-sales support and corporate culture will be discussed at length in Chapters 6 to 12. We will analyze which variables have the most influence, why many firms do poorly and what techniques our winners use to achieve superior performance.

# 5

## . . . It Begins with the Product

Customer satisfaction begins with the product. The more comfortable and convenient the product, the easier it is to use, the less it breaks down, the happier the customer is. Products that fit the customer, that act like an extension of the customer's personality, almost invariably create a high level of satisfaction. The IBM Selectric typewriter, the Xerox 914 copier, the Volkswagen Beetle—each was phenomenally successful because of its superb fit with customer needs. Using these products was an easy, satisfying, problem-free experience.

How happy customers are with a given product or service depends in part on two factors: *product design* and *product quality*. Product design affects the customer directly and tangibly. A camera that fits snugly in the hands and handles comfortably, a suit that's both elegant and functional, a golf club that balances right and swings smoothly—these are well-designed products to which consumers immediately respond favorably. Henry Dreyfuss, one of the most successful and influential designers in the United States, put it best when he said:

> What we are working on is going to be ridden in, sat upon, looked at, talked into, activated, operated, or in some way used by people individually or en masse. If the point of contact between the product and the people becomes a point of friction, then the industrial designer has failed. If, on the other hand, people are made safer, more comfortable, more eager to purchase, more efficient—or just plain happier—the designer has succeeded.

Product quality affects customer satisfaction by delivering—or not delivering—a consistent level of performance. Customers have come to expect that when they walk into a McDonald's restaurant they will find the same high quality of food, service, and cleanliness, regardless of location. Consumers similarly expect a uniformly high level of reliability from Japanese appliances and automobiles. Quality is a function of the basic design of the product or service, how well inputs are controlled, and the manufacturing or production processes used. Poor product quality can hamper even good designs, as happened with Jaguar in the 1970s and Olivetti in the United States, and will assuredly ruin poor ones, for example, Xerox's 3300 series of copiers.

What constitutes a good product? That is, how do we know when a particular product or service will keep customers happy? One answer could be that a good product has a good design. But how do we know if the design is good? Some designs may be very appealing aesthetically, yet appalling in terms of performance. Others might perform superbly, yet look like something the dog dragged in. Similarly, what do consumers mean by quality? Is it merely durability or reliability? In that case, why are Detroit cars considered of lower quality than Japanese imports? As we shall see, in terms of functional reliability there isn't much difference between Detroit and Japan.

To answer the question, "What constitutes a good product, one that will maximize customer satisfaction?" we must recognize the following:

☐ *Customers Maximize Total Value.* Consciously or subconsciously, every buyer wants the most value everywhere—in the store, in use, and in disposal.

☐ *Packaging, and Features and Functions Are Equally Important.* The common saying is, "Sizzle sells." Not quite; if you want to keep customers happy you must have both—the sizzle *and* the steak.

## TOTAL VALUE: THE KEY

The total economic value of a product to customers can be divided into three parts: its utility at the point of purchase, or *value-in-purchase*; its utility during its useful life, or *value-in-use*; and its utility at the time of disposal, or *value-in-disposal*. (See Table 5.1.)

☐ *Value-in-Purchase.* This represents the answer to the question, "How happy do I think I will be with this product or service?" The answer may be automatic, as in the case of routine purchases, such as toothpaste and toiletries, or it may the result of careful analysis of the product through trials, reading test result data, sampling, and so on. Value-in-purchase is a function of the external design or styling of the product, the communications, such as advertising and sales literature, and the atmospherics, such as how the product display is arranged and the attire of the sales personnel.

☐ *Value-in-Use.* "How happy am I with this product, now that I've bought it?" The answer determines the value-in-use of a given product or service. Such factors as the user-friendliness of the design, the balance of user-friendliness versus

**TABLE 5.1   Factors Affecting Total Value**

|  | Value-in-Purchase | Value-in-Use | Value-in-Disposal |
|---|---|---|---|
| *Packaged Goods* | Packaging Positioning | Performance Quality Safety/reliability | Ease of disposal Systems/procedures for disposal After-effects |
| *Consumer Durables* | Design Styling Hi-tech/hi-touch Channel choice | Reliability Ease of use Repair costs Overall durability | Trade-in prices Replacements Disposal systems |
| *Industrial and Business Equipment* | Design Styling Feature/functionality Hi-tech/hi-touch Channel choice | Reliability Ease of use Ease of training Duration of failures Total maintenance Expandability | Trade-in prices Upgrades/replacements Protection of existing investments in spares, software |

performance (i.e., "It's easy to use but doesn't do very much" or "It can do just about everything, once you figure out how to use it"), the after-sales support where appropriate, and the product's engineering and manufacturing quality, decide value-in-use.

☐ *Value-in-Disposal.* This is related to the question, "What do I do with this product now that I'm through with it?" This depends, again, on the design of the product, the degree to which it has a residual or salvage value, and the systems the manufacturer has set up to retrieve this salvage value.

## Values Are Determined by Costs

Although value-in-purchase is often a function of subjective criteria such as styling, appearance, and perceived or anticipated utility, all three components of total value are closely related to the costs the customer incurs. Conceptually, this is an extension of the total life-cycle cost approach firms use in making a major capital equipment purchase, in which they calculate the total cost of the equipment—purchase, installation, operator training, maintenance and repair, lost-time costs incurred by the firm because of machine failure, and disposal or salvage value—and compare this cost to the equipment's expected performance and productivity. The firm looks to maximize its performance-to-life-cycle-cost ratio. Therefore, the lower the total life-cycle cost, the higher the total value of the purchase.

This conceptual framework provides insight into the relative importance of the three components of value, as follows:

☐ *Total Value Is Related to Perceived Costs.* Other things being equal, the lower the perceived costs of the purchase, especially in use and disposal, the higher the value to the purchaser. This explains why Japanese cars remain popular despite higher price tags; buyers perceive the repair costs to be lower and resale value to be higher.

☐ *No Perceived Costs Implies No Value.* If customers do not perceive that they are incurring out-of-pocket costs because of the absence of certain features that potentially increase value in purchase, use, or disposal, they will attach very little value to these features. In that case, manufacturers cannot increase customer satisfaction by focusing on these features. Microcomputer software provides a classic example of this phenomenon. Most purchasers tend to focus on unit price and product features and usually are unwilling to pay for product support. Therefore, software vendors are finding that providing superior product support does not appreciably improve loyalty at the end-user level, as witness Lotus' difficulties with Symphony, which could not build on the large customer base of 1-2-3.

☐ *Some Costs Are External Costs.* Particularly when it comes to value-in-disposal, users often do not incur out-of-pocket costs. Society as a whole bears these costs through taxes, increased pollution, and so forth. These external costs reduce the importance of some components in determining total value.

☐ *When External Costs Are Charged Back, Total Value Changes.* When external costs become tangible, through increased insurance premiums, pollution taxes and charges, and higher

liability awards, for example, customers start including
these costs in their calculation of value. Car manufacturers
were reducing their costs by installing thinner, less durable
bumpers on automobiles. The customer tolerated this—that
is, treated it as an external cost—until repair bills for minor
collisions started to skyrocket. This led to the creation of
federal standards for bumpers.

### Customers Want the Most Total Value

Consciously or subconsciously, most consumers look for the maximum total value when choosing a product.

☐ *Purchasers of industrial machinery and business equipment* pay
careful attention to all three aspects of value—purchase,
use, and disposal. The U.S. Department of Defense requires
an explicit life-cycle cost analysis of new weapons and
equipment. Airlines similarly carry out extensive studies of
the acquisition, operating, and salvage or trade-in cost of
new aircraft.

☐ *Total value is important in real estate, automobiles,* and other
types of consumer purchases. When buying a house or con-
dominium, people want to know how close they are to the
schools, transportation, and shopping and how much maintenance will be required. In other words, they're concerned
about value-in-use. They also want to know about neighborhood property values (i.e., what the disposal, or resale,
value of their property will be).

☐ *Total value can also be important in packaged goods and in services.* Typically, packaged goods such as food and cosmetics
have a relatively short life cycle. Even in such purchases,
customers appear to be paying increasing attention to value-
in-use and value-in-disposal. Symptoms of this concern are
the greater attention paid to labeling both for content and

for nutritional value and the increasing popularity of foods that are salt-free, sugar-free, sodium-free, and so on. The controversy over phosphate-based detergents is a good example of consumer concern about disposal value; Proctor & Gamble and other detergent manufacturers were forced to remove all phosphates from detergents after the environmental outcry of the late 1960s and 1970s. Disposal value is important in services as well; for example, most home-remodeling contracts contain a clause saying that the contractor will be responsible for clearing and disposing of the waste and scrap.

### Customer Satisfaction Is Related to Total Value

Within the same price class, the higher the total value of the product, the happier the customers.

☐ *Farm Equipment.* The product's resale value is an excellent measure of the customer's overall satisfaction (see Chapter 2). Farmers value their time and effort highly. Therefore, a high price for a used machine is an indication that the purchaser believes, usually accurately, that the particular item is productive and easy to operate and may have a good resale value again. Deere recognized this early and has always paid close attention to the prices of its used equipment as an index of overall customer satisfaction.

☐ *Domestic versus Imported Automobiles.* For many years, Detroit automakers concentrated on value-in-purchase and ignored value-in-use and value-in-disposal. Their cars were not as user-friendly as those of overseas competitors, such as the Japanese. Nor did domestic cars have as much resale value as comparable Japanese and some European imports.

☐ *IBM's Experiences with the PCjr.* This is a classic example of the importance customers attach to total value. When first introduced, the PCjr had less value-in-purchase to most buyers, primarily because of such features as the "chiclet"-style keyboard and the noncompatible storage media. After IBM redesigned the keyboard, customers compared value-in-use with the then available PC clones in the same price class and decided it offered less total value because of perceived or actual compatibility problems, such as the need for program cartridges, with its mainline counterpart, the PC.

### The Relative Importance Changes

Naturally, not all customers weight the three components of value (purchase, use, and disposal) equally. For example, some car buyers look for styling, others for durability, and still others for performance. We can, however, identify certain common characteristics that determine the relative importance of the three components of value.

The nature of the purchase and the type of product often determine the degree to which buyers will look beyond value-in-purchase or showroom glitter. Broadly speaking, value-in-purchase is the driver in purchases of low-cost items, especially consumables or those with a short useful life, such as packaged goods, light bulbs, and small appliances, and items that are purchased repetitively. In purchases of items with a high unit price or a long life cycle, such as houses, major appliances, and business equipment, value-in-use and disposal or salvage value become important, sometimes much more than showroom value. If the technology is comparatively new, there will be little information regarding anything other than value-in-purchase. By contrast, other things being equal, mature products are purchased on the basis of value-in-use and resale value.

Finally, external factors can cause shifts in the relative weights. For example, so long as ecological considerations were not important, in the sense that the costs of pollution were not visible to consumers and industry, no particular importance was attached to value-in-disposal. Once these costs were made tangible through laws, consumer actions, fines, and so on, the costs of disposing of the products became an important factor in determining customer satisfaction. The fuel crises of the 1970s caused similar shifts in customer requirements regarding fuel efficiency of automobiles, appliances, furnaces, and so forth.

## PACKAGING VERSUS FEATURES AND FUNCTIONS

A friend was talking to us about his experiences with Detroit products. He had just rented a well-known luxury car.

> The parking brake hit my left shin as I got in and kept on rubbing against it all the time I had the car. The belt buckle for the seat belt was hidden inside the seat cushion; I almost caused an accident as I struggled to re-fasten it after paying for parking. I don't want to pick on [the manufacturers] . . . [Detroit] spends so much money advertising its research into ergonomics. Big deal! In every . . . car I've sat in, if I wanted to turn on the radio, I've had to lean forward. I'm average height for an American, but none of these cars fit correctly.

The car didn't *fit* right. Notice that he didn't say the car was underpowered or didn't handle correctly or had an uncomfortable ride. His dissatisfaction with the product was more subliminal: He felt that he had to adapt himself to the car, not vice versa.

People judge their satisfaction with a product along two dimensions: *packaging, and features and functions.*

☐ *Packaging.* By this we mean not only the external wrapping or styling, but also such aspects as the user-friendliness of the design—"Do I have to have a Ph.D. in engineering to use it?"; external indications of reliability—"How can I believe that it's well-made when the door won't close flush in the showroom?"; and ease of purchase—"The base price of the car is $5995, but that doesn't include the special handling package, the cloth seats, and the special trim package."

☐ *Features and Functions.* This covers product performance or capabilities—"It carries six in comfort and has a top speed of 110 mph"; range or breadth of these capabilities—"You can use this personal computer to calculate the annual income statement *and* type up the chairman's message to the shareholders"; and engineering reliability and durability—"This microprocessor chip has a mean time between failure of almost six years of continuous operation, functions flawlessly in 100° heat, and withstands 6Gs of shock."

### Packaging Makes the Difference

Repeatedly, we've found that the packaging of the product or service makes an important difference in customer satisfaction. As Tom Peters has said, "*At the margin* I will go out of my way a *little* and pay a *little* more for courtesy." The old Bell System coin telephone was solid, reassuring to the touch and simple to use. With deregulation, a number of competing coin telephones came into the market. Almost without exception, these phones are less satisfactory: They often look tacky, with garish colors and inappropriate use of chrome; their dials feel clunky or brittle to the touch, and the overall effect is extremely poor. Next time you're in an airport, take a look. You'll find the new public phones nearly deserted, while people line up to make calls on the old phones.

The problem isn't that these products don't do the job; the new coin telephones certainly work. What makes customers unhappy is the manner in which the job is done. They resent the fact that the product is not user-friendly, that they have to adapt to the product instead of the product adapting to their needs.

When customers have few choices—in a monopoly, for instance—they can do little more than grin and bear it. However, the moment a more user-oriented product appears on the scene, buyers switch their loyalties. Because VisiCalc was the first spreadsheet available on a microcomputer, it captured a large number of customers. However, the program was not user-friendly: It was difficult to use, its output could not be easily combined into a word-processing program, and the user had to work hard to produce graphics, such as bar charts and pie charts, from the spreadsheet. Therefore, when Lotus introduced its 1-2-3 program, which was user-friendly, the product was an overnight success despite its higher price.

Packaging becomes particularly important as competition in an industry heats up or when a technology matures. In these circumstances, customers find it difficult to choose among competing products on the basis of features or capabilities; all the products do the job. Buyers therefore switch their attention to other aspects of the product, such as ease of use, perceived quality, and ease of purchase. In other words, the focus of buyer interest and of competition shifts from features and functions to packaging.

### Fits and Finishes

The automotive industry offers one of the most vivid examples of the importance of packaging in determining customer perceptions and satisfaction. In the public mind, Japanese imports are built better, are more reliable, and provide better value for money. This is certainly reflected in customer satisfaction with Japanese cars. In J.D. Power and Associates' 1985 annual survey of customer satisfaction, 9 out of the top 10 nameplates were imports, and 4 of these were Japanese.

However, if we analyze data about quality, reliability, and durability, as Abernathy, Clark, and Kantrow did in their classic analysis of the U.S. automotive industry, we find:

> In terms of *mechanical* reliability—the reliability of engine, drive-train, electrical systems, brakes, exhausts, suspension, and so forth—Japanese and U.S. automobiles are about even (Table 5.2);
>
> Japanese cars appeared to rust out a little faster, based on 1981 data.
>
> Further, a 1984 J.D. Power survey indicated that average, median annual maintenance costs for U.S. cars ($93) are significantly less than those for Japanese imports ($133) and almost one-third of those for European cars ($246).

Then what makes consumers feel that Japanese cars are more reliable? The answer is their fits and finishes. (See Table 5.3.) Japanese automobiles look better in the showroom, based on how cus-

TABLE 5.2  *Ratings of Reliability of U.S. and Japanese Cars (1981)*[a]

| Country/Model | Mechanical |
|---|---|
| United States | |
|   Chevrolet Chevette | 9.6 |
|   Volkswagen Rabbit | 10.0 |
|   Dodge Omni | 9.6 |
|   Ford Escort | 9.6 |
| Japan | |
|   Toyota Corolla | 12.3 |
|   Honda Civic | 11.9 |
|   Mitsubishi Colt | 11.2 |
|   Datsun 210 | 10.8 |
|   Mazda GLC | 9.6 |

[a]The numbers represented are average ratings of frequency of repair, as made by readers of *Consumer Reports*. The numbers are based on a scoring system, ranging from 0 to 20 as follows: 0 = Far Below Average, 10 = Average, 20 = Far Above Average.

*Source: Consumer Reports* (April 1982).

**TABLE 5.3   Evidence on Workmanship: A Comparison of U.S. and Japanese Automobiles (1979)**

| Country/Model | Consumer Ratings[a] (condition of car at delivery) | Defects per Vehicle Shipped (after one month) |
|---|---|---|
| United States | | |
|   Chevrolet Chevette | 7.2 | 3.00 |
|   Ford Pinto | 6.5 | 3.70 |
|   Volkswagen Rabbit | 7.8 | 2.13 |
|   Dodge Omni | 7.4 | 4.10 |
|   Plymouth Horizon | 7.5 | n/a |
| Japan | | |
|   Toyota Corolla | 7.8 | 0.71[b] |
|   Honda Civic | 8.0 | 1.23[c] |
|   Mitsubishi Colt | 7.8 | n/a |

[a]Scale of 1 to 10; 10 = excellent.
[b]Toyota average.
[c]Honda average.
Source: Rogers National Research, *Buyer Profiles*, 1979; discussions with industry executives.

tomers rate the car at the time of delivery, and a month later have far fewer problems, compared with their Detroit counterparts. Basically, Japanese cars are put together with more attention to items that affect *perceived* reliability and quality—the fits and finishes—such as paint quality, rattles and squeaks, water leaks, noise, body alignment, and window seals. In terms of what the industry calls "showroom quality," the Japanese have been ahead of Detroit for nearly two decades.

## WHY PRODUCTS FAIL TO SATISFY

Why do companies design products that are awkward to use, aren't reliable, or wear out quickly? Why don't companies design and manufacture products that maximize total value and customer satisfaction?

Firms don't set out to design bad products. In the transition from the drawing board to the showroom floor, however, companies make design changes and compromises that ultimately reduce customer satisfaction.

The real issue is, once again, the trade-off companies make between cost and customer. In many cases, cost wins. Unlike what our friend with the rented car believes, it is likely that someone at Chrysler knows that the parking brake rubs against the driver's left shin and that the seat belts are awkward to buckle. However, the company has made the trade-off in favor of cost reduction. Undoubtedly, at some point management decided it was too expensive to revise the design to move the parking brake; the molding would have to be changed and new tooling bought. A company repeats this process of compromise until what started out as a good design is transformed into a barely satisfactory one.

In addition to the overall cost-focus, companies make the following mistakes where the product is concerned:

- ☐ They don't think beyond the point of sale.
- ☐ They don't ensure that design, manufacturing, and marketing all understand what customers want.
- ☐ They don't go below the surface when designing products.
- ☐ They don't provide proper feedback to designers and manufacturing.
- ☐ They don't have a top-management commitment to customer satisfaction.

### They Don't Think Beyond the Point of Sale

All too often, companies concentrate on trying to maximize value-in-purchase and ignore value-in-use and value-in-disposal. When designing and packaging the product, they fail to think of the customer's needs after the sale. In some cases they may not even maximize value at the point of sale; Detroit automakers are an example of companies with this failing. In contrast, people feel comfortable in a Japanese car, because the Japanese have learned that to maximize customer satisfaction, they must think beyond the buying stage.

### They Don't Know What Customers Want

More precisely, these companies do not create a clear, unified and coherent picture of customers' wants and needs in the design, engineering, manufacturing, and marketing divisions. The result is that each function has its own perspective on what keeps customers happy. What is worse, in many cases these perspectives may not be based on what customers actually want, but rather on the division's own priorities or interests. Often this leads to an engineer designing a product that is better from an engineering point of view but that fails to meet fundamental customer needs.

Even firms that usually design good products are not immune to this syndrome. In the early 1980s, Xerox had to make major changes in its design teams' attitudes before it could address some of the problems that customers perceived. For example, when marketing reported an extremely high level of dissatisfaction with the frequency of paper jams on one model of copier, the engineering division's reaction was one of disbelief. Engineers argued that the customers were wrong, because the Xerox model jammed no more frequently than did comparable competitive models. "They just weren't getting the message," David Ely of Xerox said. Even after he gave a presentation stressing the importance of understanding and satisfying the customer, Ely said, one engineer declared that the machine he designed had an ongoing-maintenance rating "as good as or better than all the competition out there, and I can't help it if the customer doesn't like it."

### They Don't Go Below the Surface

In many firms, design is equated with skin-deep styling. Detroit's designs in the 1950s are the example *par excellence* of this approach—tailfins, lots of chrome, and lots of glitter. In contrast to the European approach, in which form follows function, many U.S. companies pay very little attention to the internal functioning, ease of use, or ease of repair. How else can we explain the fact that in a Detroit product of the late 1970s, you had to jack up the engine to reach two of the sparkplugs? Or that on a major trunk airline, passengers in the frequent-flyer program don't get credit for mileage on a flight if they fail to present their coupons when they board? As Henry Dreyfus put it, "I prefer the concept of 'cleanlining,' in which a streamlined appearance is directly related to function. . . . Stand a 1929 toaster, with its knobs and knuckle-skinning corners and impossible-to-clean slits and overall ugliness, next to today's model, and the difference is apparent."

### They Don't Provide Feedback

Companies often do not provide feedback regarding customer concerns and complaints to all the functions involved in developing and marketing a product. Consequently, the designer proceeds to make the same mistakes over and over again. In the case of Xerox, the firm for many years had no formal system for letting engineers know what the customer thought of the product. Often, within a large company, intracompany communications are so poor that lessons learned from one division are not accepted or implemented by another. Ford's experience with the Escort is a classic example. In 1980, Ford of Europe launched a redesigned version of the Escort which was a stunning success. The appearance of the car was changed from a boxy, rather frumpy design to one that was sleek and highly functional—a precursor of the way the Ford Taurus and the Mercury Sable look. But the U.S. designers had little confidence in the European design team. Consequently, they insisted on reengineering the car totally; as a result, it became boxier, heavier, less fuel efficient, and less satisfactory to handle.

### They Don't Have Top Management Commitment

This usually is at the root of the problem. In many large, multidivision companies, senior management no longer identifies personally with the products. Consequently, there is very little of the old craftsman's pride in making a good product. When this pride is lacking at the top, it inevitably leads to a more casual attitude toward design and customer satisfaction. As discussed earlier, senior management increasingly comes to rely on objective measures of customer satisfaction—opinion polls, percentiles, and statistics. Managers lose their appreciation for that intangible element in product design and development that leads to superior satisfaction. It is no coincidence, in our view, that Ford's resurgence, as represented by the Sable and the Taurus, came under the leadership of 'Red' Poling (former president of Ford), who was personally interested and involved in design.

## HOW THE WINNERS DO IT

The firms in our survey—the winners—consistently create products and services that excel at satisfying their customers. Mercedes-Benz, Subaru, and Jaguar owners rate their cars very high in terms of performance. International travelers rate Swissair's services, both on the ground and in the air, as their key reason for rating Swissair number one in customer satisfaction. Similarly, Xerox copiers' features and performance rate very high on user surveys.

As might be expected, *how* they achieve this varies considerably from company to company depending on the technologies involved, industry characteristics, the types of customers to which they market their products, and the internal culture of the companies. For example: Xerox uses extensive surveys to define customer needs and a highly structured product development system. Boeing organizes working groups of customer personnel—pilots, maintenance engineers, and ground crew—to view proposed new designs every step of the way. By contrast, Deere's style is much more informal, almost deceptively casual.

Beneath these superficial differences in style and processes, the following common characteristics were found which we believe are key to explaining these firms' success in consistently designing and manufacturing products and services that satisfy:

☐ Their design, engineering, and manufacturing personnel know customer needs intimately.

☐ They create internal alliances during product development.

☐ They create customer alliances during product development.

☐ They want their products and services to beat BOB (best of breed).

☐ They have strong, responsive customer feedback systems.

☐ They provide incentives to designers and manufacturing for improving customer satisfaction.

☐ They are constantly innovating or improving their products to increase customer satisfaction.

## DESIGNERS AND ENGINEERS KNOW THE CUSTOMER INTIMATELY

In each of these companies, designers, engineers, and often the manufacturing personnel work very hard at getting close to the customer. This has two immediate benefits: First, it ensures that the designers of a product are keenly aware of and alert to the needs, concerns, and idiosyncrasies of various users without having these interpreted to them by the marketing function. By getting close to the customer, the designers and engineers eliminate the marketing filter with its conscious and unconscious biases. In turn, this makes it easier for marketing to communicate the exact needs of the marketplace when designing new products or modifying existing ones. We believe that this closeness to the customer on the part of designers and engineers, more than any other characteristic, is the key reason why these firms' products provide high levels of satisfaction. Sometimes this knowledge of the customer within the engineering and manufacturing divisions is part and parcel of the heritage of the company. This certainly appears to have been the situation at Deere. Russ Sutherland, vice president of Engineering and the man responsible for directing Deere's overall product development, put it thus, "I think that this is an area where we have had strength in the past partly because of where we were and who we were. If you go back to when I started with the company, and you went into the product engineering department, that center of gravity was around an engineer who was born and raised on a farm. So he kind of intuitively thought like a farmer. Chances are his dad was one, and he probably had something on the side, on weekends, anyhow." He goes on to add that, "Today this is no longer possible due to the fact that fewer and fewer of Deere's engineers have a farm background. Consequently, Deere has had to implement relatively formalized procedures to capture something that we almost knew by instinct we had."

In this respect, Deere was significantly different from its competitors. "If I stop and think of who our competitors were 35 years ago, it was International Harvester, based in Chicago, with a truck division and a cream separator division and a refrigerator division and an air-conditioner division, and I suspect there was at least some movement back and forth between them at headquarters, Michigan Avenue. And one of the major competitors was Massey-Ferguson, headquarters in Detroit; matter of fact,

practically all of their engineering was done in the Detroit area."
While he did not say it in so many words, there is no doubt that
Sutherland believes the farm background of Deere's engineers
has been an important factor in Deere's success.

Nor is this restricted to the design engineers; Deere's manufacturing personnel also have (or work to acquire) a sound knowledge
of the farmer. Further, Deere even arranges visits by factory
workers to farms so that the average assembly-line workers—
who today may not have the same farm background as their fa-
thers did—get to know the customers, and their needs and concerns, at least vicariously.

While it may sound simple, keeping engineers and designers
close to the customer is not easy to do. Part of the reason is that,
by and large, these individuals aren't necessarily concerned about
what the *external* customer wants; their background, training, and
professional culture tend to make them primarily concerned
about the mechanics of a product—how it works, how it extends
the state-of-the-art, how many different functions it can perform,
and so forth. Changing this internal orientation often takes a considerable investment in time and resources, as Xerox found out in
the early 1980s. Kerney Ladey, vice president of National Service,
who was deeply involved in the efforts to make Xerox more responsive to the customer, discussed some of the problems he encountered: "I spent a year [at the factory] coming from marketing
and I went there to do two things. One, was to provide some insight to the engineering world about what customers think about
machines. . . . At that time they [the engineers and designers]
were more interested in making whatever the mechanics they
were doing work to their satisfaction. It was more internal than it
was external, and they were more interested in trying to make
sure that it [the machine] ran to their specification." He goes on to
add that, in his opinion, the major problem was the engineers
and designers recognizing who the output was for—in other
words, who the customer really was. In his view, "[customer] orientation hadn't begun yet, and so, for that reason, they were en-

amored with, how complex does it make it? How could you make it have so many wheels that they all turn around at the same time? versus Is it going to be pertinent to the customer, or will it take an engineer to fix it? We had lots of discussions about that." In order to change this internal focus, Xerox has used a combination of extensive customer surveys, focus groups, and other techniques. For example: They brought customers in and went through some exploratory interviews in which customers aired their dissatisfactions and problems with various products. These were videotaped and later the videotape was replayed in front of the engineers. As David Ely of Xerox put it, "We had twelve of these in a row . . . and that got their attention. The company even brought in service engineers who were supporting the customer to talk with designers and tell them where the problems were and what the customers were saying. The end result of these efforts is a nine-step process that Xerox uses for all products to maximize customer satisfaction."

When this process works well, the company knows its customers so well that, without meaning to, it may at times sound almost arrogant. As Karl Faber, vice president of Mercedes-Benz, says, "We do what we think is right for the customer, for example, the air bag. One customer was afraid to drive the car with an air bag; after two weeks he had forgotten it was there. In the long run, customers will realize that they have bought something for their benefit. We started the air bag as an option in 1983. We're still losing money on our investment but we believe we did the right thing."

## THEY CREATE INTERNAL ALLIANCES

Each of these firms creates internal alliances between the design, manufacturing, service, and marketing divisions. These alliances operate almost as a second channel, swifter and more effective than formal company channels, providing feedback from marketing to engineering, or from engineering to manufacturing, and so on. As a result, in these firms people don't wait until things have reached crisis proportions before they act. Instead, what we found was a constant flow of information from the customer back to design and manufacturing, and a stream of small but steady product changes.

These alliances obviously don't occur overnight; in most cases they were the result of conscious attention by management. In some cases, these alliances have evolved over time fostered by the culture of the company and the backgrounds of the individuals. At Deere, for example, the Midwestern, rural backgrounds of many managers has formed an invisible bond which has been reinforced by careful rotation of key individuals across engineering, manufacturing, marketing, and service. This has been supplanted by extended assignments on task forces that work and, equally important, travel as a group. At Swissair the common bond is the ancient tradition of Swiss hospitality. This appears to infect all Swissair employees—whether they are Swiss nationals or foreigners. In fact, according to Bernard Oettli, general manager, customer service, "the latter almost become more Swiss than the Swiss!" This common bond is reinforced by employee selection, rotation, and promotion policies. At the time of hiring, Swissair does personality screening looking for those personalities that "will fit into the company culture of putting the customer first, being patient, not being authoritative, not trying to be bossy." This is followed by a long probation period. This customer orientation is reinforced in the promotion system. For example, in filling openings for the purser position (the first level of supervision) candidates are evaluated on the basis of three factors: one-third on professional knowledge, one-third on a psychological examination, and the final third what Oettli called "the footprint someone left in the company, meaning what do his or her superiors think, what is the impression he or she left, [what was his/her] previous performance."

Whatever the methods, the end result of creating such internal alliances is a group of people who know each other very well and who have a common set of values and beliefs. This enables the entire organization to better translate customer needs into specific products and services. Ideally, both engineering and marketing must understand the nature of the compromises necessary to create products that both maximize customer satisfaction and yet provide a reasonable profit. For this to occur, each side must have a clear appreciation of the problems and concerns of the other functions. As Ladey of Xerox put it, "they [the engineers] taught me a lot about what you have to do to build a product and what some of the limitations were, what trade-offs you have to make, what emphasis they place in terms of delivering those three elements of quality I mentioned. I was able to take that and understand from this job some of the pressure points they [the engineers and designers] were under, and it gave me a pretty good feel for the interaction that I need to have with them."

One of the most important benefits of these internal alliances is that they enable the various functions—engineering, manufacturing, production planning, service, and so on—to optimize the total system. In other words, by involving the various functions from the very beginning, the result will be a product that not only does the job, but is easy to manufacture, easy to service, and, of course, easy to use; to use our terminology, a product that maximizes total customer value. In many cases, things about the product that dissatisfy customers—poor instructions, awkward or difficult to use controls, and so forth—are due to this lack of communication between the various functions.

## THEY CREATE CUSTOMER ALLIANCES

When developing products and services, our winners also work to establish a sense of partnership with customers (i.e., they try to build customer alliances). This is consistent with their overall win–win approach to the customer. While this is easy to do and understandable for industrial equipment companies such as Boeing and Xerox, consumer products firms, such as Kodak, Kraft, and Whirlpool, also go to great lengths to create this sense of identity and ownership within their customers.

The benefits of such customer alliances are obvious. First, a close working relationship with a customer ensures prompt feedback of customer concerns. Correcting these problems strengthens the relationship—the customer is happier with the product and therefore buys more from the company, which increases profits, which further motivates the company to respond quickly to customer needs. Customers are also the best source for new product ideas—a fact that has long been recognized in industrial marketing. Finally, a close working relationship with the customer ensures that the company will not be caught unawares by any shifts in customer tastes and needs.

Some of the ways in which Kraft creates an alliance with its customers are described by Dean Nelson of Kraft Foodservice, "Several of our major chain accounts . . . are very interested in having us sit down with them and talk about what's happening in the food industry in the United States. Not strictly from a food service standpoint, [but rather] what's happening in retail, what are the trends in the grocery stores, what does the American consumer think? So we do that with our customers. . . . Also, our research and development center is an added plus for us because we work very closely with [the customer's] product development team."

Boeing's experiences provide a vivid example of the problems and the benefits of building such a customer alliance. As Jim Blue, a vice president at Boeing, put it, "We take pride in the fact that we are market driven, but that is not an easy position to maintain. It's much easier to design a product [internally] . . . and not go through what is usually a very painful process of exposing that product to the customers for their comments. We try very hard, particularly during our design process, to involve the customer. Sometimes we do it very well and sometimes not as well. That is a painful process, because essentially what you do is take it to the customer and say, 'Here is what we think is good,' and they say, 'Yes, but . . . ' or 'No, it is not . . . ' or show you the shortcomings. You clearly have to be working with a customer who perceives that there is a reasonable likelihood that he will buy the product. If you just go ask for opinions, what everybody would like is an airplane that doesn't burn any fuel at all, goes an infinite distance, and carries 5000 people; so 'like' is not the issue. The issue is that set of very complex [trade-offs] that end up in a good design."

Clearly Boeing feels that the benefits of these customer alliances outweigh the difficulties of making it work. These difficulties should not be understated. For example, what eventually became the Boeing 727 started out as a twin-engine plane, which is what Eastern wanted. United, on the other hand, wanted a four-engine plane to meet its high altitude requirements at Denver. While the compromise—three engines—seems almost obvious in retrospect, it was extremely difficult to obtain.

Boeing's experiences with the 727 also illustrate the benefits of a strong customer alliance. Blue said, "We are lucky in that we've got customers who have all sorts of requirements: United with Denver, Mexicana with Mexico City, Eastern with places such as Miami—hot and humid. We've got relatively long-range requirements in the United States. So that by trying to please all of those customers you are forced to arrive at some compromises that probably make the airplane better. In contrast, [look at] what was then the Hawker Siddeley Trident: same basic layout, same technical characteristics, but [the airline] setting the requirements was . . . British European Airways. They didn't have a long-range requirement, no high altitude airports, no really hot-day requirements, so the airplane came out far less capable than the 727. I think that showed in the ultimate market success of the product."

This strong customer alliance not only makes existing or proposed products better and more satisfying, it often helps the firm identify new opportunities in advance of the competition. For example, it was Kodak's strong alliance with its customers—dealers and end-users—that helped the firm identify the needs that led to the disk camera. As John Barnes, Kodak's vice president of customer and marketing support, views it, "In the United States, it's no secret that 85 percent or more of all households have at least one camera. In those households there's a heavy report of Kodak equipment, a wide variety, from roll-film cameras to cartridge cameras, pocket cameras, and the like. Our mission was to find out, despite the fact that we had smaller, more compact, easy-to-use cameras, 'Why aren't you, Mr. and Mrs. America, taking more pictures? Is there something that we can do to cause picture taking to be easier for you?' A very exhaustive survey was made and it came out again, very clear: 'You say you have simple, easy-to-use, pocket cameras, but let me tell you, you're a long way away from you push the button, we do the rest.' "

What Kodak discovered was that in the operation of even its simplest cameras to date, there were probably nine thought(s)/finger strokes that were necessary in order to take a picture. In other words, while the company believed that photography was easy, the customer was saying it wasn't. According to Barnes, "The proof of the pudding is in the yield (the number of usable pictures available from one roll) . . . in the disk [camera], you get almost 100 percent yield—14.7 pictures out of 15. [By contrast] in pocket cameras the yield is probably down in the 80 to 85 percent range. I have even seen it as low as 75. . . . With the disk you can't make a mistake. It does everything, literally, but take the picture for you, but it keeps you sufficiently involved that it's of interest to you."

## BEATING BOB

Buck Rodgers, former vice president of marketing at IBM, recalls, "When IBM does comparisons it's done against what is called the best of breed. You just don't want to say here is an average sampling of product capability and the strengths . . . but rather, you pick those competitors who you think possess the greatest price performance, the greatest innovation in their products, and so on and that's what you compare yourself against."

As Rodgers illustrates, the winners want their products to beat BOB, Best of Breed. In other words, they worked hard to ensure that their products and services were better than the *best* in that particular category.

Their reasons for wanting to beat BOB are twofold: First, these firms want to be sure that whatever they make and sell provides the greatest value available in the market to the customer. In part, this reflects their pride—a Kodak, an IBM, a Swissair doesn't want to be second to anyone. But it also ensures that these firms will retain their leadership position in the customer's minds.

The second reason for wanting to beat BOB is to ensure that managers don't lose sight of the original goal—keeping the customer happy—as the product moves from concept to reality. In a competitive marketplace firms are always under pressure to cut product costs—do less, build it a little cheaper, make it more profitable. By holding up the goal "beat BOB" these firms ensure that the end result still maximizes customer satisfaction.

They determine the best of breed by talking to customers and finding out who in the customer's opinion provides the best performance on various product dimensions; for example, who has the most reliability, ease of use, range of features, and so on. Then, internal products are compared against this best of breed along each dimension, usually with the help of impartial evaluators. Typically, products that do not meet or beat BOB along key dimensions are sent back to the drawing board; there's no compromising on standards.

## TIGHT FEEDBACK LOOPS

Each of our winners uses tight feedback loops. They are able to locate and define the problems customers are having with a particular product or service very early, bring it to the attention of the relevant people or functions, solve them, and get customer satisfaction back on track quickly. Overall, their response time to customer dissatisfaction appears to be significantly higher than that of their competitors. As a result, these firms are able to:

Diffuse problems with the product early, before they snowball and really create havoc, and

Make any changes necessary to the design as quickly and cost effectively as possible.

These tight feedback loops also appear to have additional, intangible benefits. They help minimize finger pointing and, instead, enable the various functions to concentrate on the main objective: keeping the customer happy. By providing quick, timely feedback to design and engineering, they ensure that the mistakes of previous products are not repeated.

Swissair is an excellent case of a tight feedback loop with internal systems and procedures for responding to any problems. Every month, Swissair surveys customers to find out what they think of key aspects of its service. This is a scientific survey designed to take account of differences in route lengths, destinations, departure times, classes of travel, and so forth. The results are tabulated exhaustively and presented every quarter to all key executives. These reports highlight, for all to see, any part of Swissair that is departing from the corporate goal of fewer than 3 percent of customers surveyed rating Swissair as fair or poor. The value of this feedback loop can be seen from the two anecdotes outlined in the next sections.

### Skydreamer? Forget it!

In the middle of the second quarter of 1982, Swissair introduced a 51 inch pitch seat—the Skydreamer—to counter the appeal of the Slumberette seats offered by other airlines—especially Pan

Am and TWA—in first-class. Within three months, they found that their customers hated the Skydreamer; this was discovered through the monthly survey reports. (See Figure 5.1.) Consequently, Swissair had to retrofit all of its first-class cabins with the industry-standard Slumberettes.

### Bread versus Booze

Another hilarious example concerns the satisfaction with drink service on a flight to Scandinavia. As Oettli of Swissair recalls, "It's an evening flight. We managed with a lot of things on the DC9-51 to keep the dissatisfaction level somewhere around 7 percent and then we changed the aircraft type [to the DC9-81]. We had another configuration, and another crew system, and that hadn't been planned too well—especially not for this flight to Stockholm. That was in January. In February we had the first month of DC9-81 operations, and in March the second one, and our complaint rate went up to 15 percent and then to 25 percent

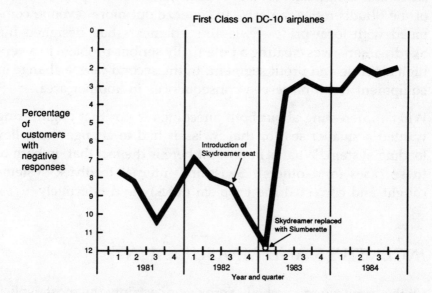

*Figure 5.1 Swissair customer satisfaction surveys for introduction of sky-dreamer seat*

within two months." The problem was, "The first system that we started with was that people would just get their meal, and then could ask for their drink at the same time." Oettli continued, "This wasn't enough for them. They really wanted it beforehand, and it was just a two-hour flight. It's an interesting point . . . because [the passengers are] a mixture of Swiss and Scandinavians. The Scandinavians don't care that much about the food. They would be quite content with some cold cuts and a little bit of fish, as long as they get their drinks. But we have Swiss customers, too, and they are a bit fussy about the food; they like a hot meal in the evening. What we did then was to form a task force of pursers and send them on all these flights. They figured out what we should change, and they came back, and then we introduced special briefings." To meet customer needs, Swissair had to change the catering, the galley loading system, and cabin crew training in order that drinks followed by a hot meal could all be served in the space of a short flight.

Both of these anecdotes indicate, in microcosm, the kinds of pressures that continually affect product design/delivery. In the case of the Slumberettes, a desire to squeeze out more revenue combined with local pride—Swissair's engineers had designed the Skydreamer—was creating a potentially serious problem in a very high revenue and profit segment. In the second case, a change in equipment had unforeseen consequences in another area.

What's interesting about both anecdotes is not that engineering wanted a smaller seat or that Swissair had to change the galley loading system. What is important here is the fact that, in both of these cases (and others), Swissair's internal feedback systems caught and corrected the problem quickly and effectively.

## INCENTIVES AND MEASUREMENTS

Of the firms we researched, Xerox was certainly the most explicit in using incentives based on customer satisfaction to measure and reward managerial performance. The others used a combination of detailed measurements and more informal rewards and sanctions. Sometimes, these were embedded in the culture of the firm; several of our winners indicated that "people around here realize that the best way to get ahead in this firm is to pay attention to the customer, and conversely, a surefire way to fail is to ignore or, worse yet, hide any customer problems." Or, as Dr. Samuel Johnson once put it, "The prospect of being hanged in the morning concentrates a man's mind wonderfully."

In other cases firms used peer pressure to improve customer satisfaction by providing extensive feedback to all departments. Subaru's David Wager provides a vivid illustration: "On a very frequent [basis], we will take videotape recorders down to the port and survey the cars. . . . If we find any kind of problems with the cars, including the fact that there's not enough gas to get the car off the boat, or a battery that won't start, there's a videotape made with the serial number and someone explaining in English and in Japanese what the problem is. That videotape is duplicated and immediately airfreighted back to Japan where the actual management is the actual technicians that worked on the cars, see these videotapes. . . . [K]nowing the Japanese as I do . . . they sure don't want to see that they made a mistake, and certainly in front of their peers, to watch, 'By the way, we checked the serial number [and] you, Mr. Ito, are responsible for this mistake.' "

## THEY NEVER STOP INNOVATING

In the 1960s Volkswagen used to run an advertisement that said, in effect, "Here's a list of the 267 changes we've made to this year's Beetle," while showing a car that appeared to be identical to last year's model. Some of this was certainly advertising tactics aimed at creating and maintaining buyer interest in a car that changed very little externally from one year to the next. But it also reflected Volkswagen's determination to constantly improve its cars and to provide ever-higher levels of satisfaction. Certainly, this had to be a major factor in the durability of the design and in Volkswagen's phenomenal success in the U.S. market; at one point, Volkswagen *was* the import car market.

The firms we interviewed showed a similar determination to keep improving their products, regardless of their age or what new products were going to be introduced in the near future. At Maytag, for example, to quote Art Heimann, Maytag's chief manufacturing engineer, "We try to find modes in which the product will fail so we can feed that back to the designers. We run lifecycle tests on all products throughout the entire manufacturing life of the product. As a matter of fact, we were still running tests on the wringer washer until we discontinued it recently." Maytag first started making wringer washers in 1907 and only discontinued them in 1983!

The reason for this constant innovation—some might call it tinkering—lies in the "impossibly" high standards these companies set for themselves and their refusal to "value engineer" or cut corners on their products. These firms appear to attract, and even encourage, perfectionists who keep pushing to see how the product could be improved further. The internal ethos of setting and achieving high standards reinforces this behavior. And the refusal to value engineer the product—to say that if it meets 70 to 80 percent of customer needs with only 20 to 30 percent of the effort, there's no need to spend the additional resources—ensures that employees will not feel inhibited about suggesting and implementing changes that, however small, stand a chance of improving customer satisfaction.

# 6

# *Understanding and Managing Customer Expectations*

What customers expect of your products and services in terms of performance, convenience, and value has a profound effect on their overall satisfaction with your company. If their expectations are unrealistically high, nothing you do will satisfy them; consequently they will always be simmering mutinously. On the other hand, if they don't expect very much, only a few masochists will buy your products. Therefore, in order to keep customers happy you must understand and control their expectations regarding your products and services.

Most firms spend considerable sums of money researching customer expectations. However, few appreciate the degree to which these expectations are affected by:

How they advertise their products,

The atmospherics that are present at the point of sale,

The attitudes of their salesforce and/or intermediaries, and

How the actual sale is conducted.

Lacking this understanding, firms misuse customer expectations for short-term profits by overpromising, overselling, managing customers' needs badly, concealing or denying poor performance, and so forth. The net result is that, in many cases, buyers' ideas regarding the performance of the product, its capabilities, and the value it represents are very different from what the manufacturer of the product assumed them to be, leading inevitably to unhappy, disgruntled customers.

The firms in our survey stood out from the rest in their understanding of how customers' needs are affected by the firm's actions. Each of these companies was extremely careful about the expectations it created, in order to ensue that customers were not oversold. They controlled atmospherics, sales attitudes, and incentives closely. They communicated extensively with customers, alerting them about potential problems before they occurred as well as fine tuning expectations to ensure that they would be consistent with what the firm could reliably deliver. Finally, they emphasized the importance of meeting customer commitments, almost regardless of cost.

## EXPECTATIONS AFFECT SATISFACTION

The receptionist says, "The doctor will be with you in five minutes." When, 35 minutes later, you're greeted with a cheerful, "And how are *we* today?," you're disappointed and irritable. When your secretary says "I FedEx'ed™ the contract yesterday," you feel confident about calling the other party at 11 in the morning to discuss changes. The late-paying account has just said,

"The check's in the mail"; when you receive an envelope containing the payment, you breathe a sigh of relief.

These three situations graphically illustrate how communications affect expectations and, in turn, customer satisfaction. You're disappointed with the doctor because his performance (35 minutes late) was below your expectations (five minutes). You're satisfied with Federal Express because they kept their promise by delivering the contract before 10:30 the next morning. Finally, when the late-paying client paid more than you'd expected, you were happy.

Customers judge their satisfaction or dissatisfaction with a product by comparing its performance against a reference level of expectations that they've created or that has been established in their minds. If performance is below expectations, they're dissatisfied or unhappy; if performance equals expectations, they're satisfied; and if performance exceeds expectations, they're very happy. Conceptually, we can say that

$$\text{Customer satisfaction} = \frac{\text{Performance}}{\text{Expectations}}$$

Therefore we can keep customers happy in one of two ways: We can work to make certain that the performance of our products exceeds their expectations. Alternatively, we can lower the expectations of customers about our products so that they're satisfied with whatever we provide!

## HOW COMPANIES CAN AFFECT EXPECTATIONS

Customers' expectations are created and modified by past experience, information they receive from the firm, feedback from other customers, competitors, news media, third parties such as regulatory agencies and consumer groups, and, on occasion, their experiences with newer technologies used in other products. While the relative importance of these forces varies considerably by industry, the firm usually plays an important role in creating and modifying its customers' expectations.

Firms condition customers' expectations directly through their advertising—both media and content—and indirectly through their use or misuse of atmospherics, sales attitudes and incentives, and sales performance.

- ☐ *Advertising.* Firms have to maintain a fine balance between raising expectations high enough so that the customer is interested enough to try the product and raising expectations so high that they are unattainable, thereby guaranteeing dissatisfaction. TWA's recent advertising campaign slogan, "Find out how good we *really* are!"™ is a perfect example of this dilemma. TWA needed to revive passengers' confidence in its ability to provide reliable, comfortable service. However, TWA also needed to be very careful to be sure that it could really deliver the goods. If, after hearing the slogans and watching the advertisements, customers found that nothing much had changed, the company would be much worse off! Passengers whose expectations had been raised by the advertising would be much more disappointed and much less likely to fly the airline again in the near future.

- ☐ *Media Selection.* How the advertisement is delivered also affects customers' ideas about the product. Prime-time TV advertisements are generally more credible than those shown during off-peak periods, while UHF TV advertisements are often viewed with deep suspicion. When introducing Courier Pak™, the first guaranteed overnight package delivery service, Federal Express deliberately spent large sums on prime time, nationwide TV commercials, and print advertisements in premier newspapers. It wanted to establish its credibility with customers and convince them that it could, indeed, deliver the package "absolutely, positively overnight."

Nearly all firms are aware of these direct means of affecting customer expectations. However, they tend to underestimate the impact of the following, indirect influences:

☐ *Atmospherics.* The layout, decor, color schemes, cleanliness, noise level—in short all the environmental factors that go into creating the atmosphere at the point of purchase—have a tremendous impact on what customers expect of your products. The slightly sloppy air of the typical greasy spoon immediately lowers our expectations about its cooking; we simply don't expect (and very rarely get) Julia Child performing in the kitchen. The same holds for most major airport restaurants and snack shops, with the added insult of high prices. On the other hand, our expectations are raised when we walk into a McDonald's, or are greeted by a Federal Express delivery person, or shake hands with a CENTURY 21® realtor. Each of these firms is using the atmospherics to raise and control our expectations about their products and services.

☐ *Sales Attitudes and Incentives.* Customers judge the company by the sales personnel it keeps. If they're friendly and interested in keeping the customer happy, buyers feel the company will be, too. On the other hand, if the salesperson projects insincerity or lack of concern about customer satisfaction, purchasers assume the worst about the firm and its products. Thus sales attitudes and incentives play a very important role in setting customers' expectations. Auto dealerships are a classic example of poor attitudes and incentives in sales—a volume orientation, incentive pressures to load up the customer with unnecessary options, no incentives for good after-sales support, service technicians paid on flat-rate basis at so much per type of repair, and so forth. Therefore it is no surprise that customers have little loyalty to their dealer; they simply don't expect very much and show it by their actions. The car dealership profession has been used as a metaphor for dishonesty in other professions—remember the 1960 election campaign slogan, "Would you buy a used car from *this* man?"

☐ *Sales Performance.* How the salesperson executes and follows through on the sale also has an important effect on customer expectations. A major reason for IBM's success lies in the fact that its salesforce is trained to sell consultatively—sell a solution rather than a particular system. This creates a positive impression in customers' minds by reinforcing IBM's interest in customer satisfaction. Under such conditions, customers are more likely to believe sales promises and assurances; instinctively, they feel that the salesperson and the salesperson's company will deliver.

## MOST COMPANIES MISMANAGE EXPECTATIONS

Our research suggests that the majority of firms fail to understand the importance of controlling or managing customers' expectations. That's putting it mildly; in many cases companies create their own problems by generating unrealistic expectations and ruining their credibility with customers. They pump up short-term sales by overpromising and overselling. They try to manage expectations dishonestly. And they work hard to hide bad news, rather than face facts and deal with the problem.

### They Overpromise

Firms often hype their products or services through advertising to create expectations far above what can be realistically delivered.

☐ *Financial Services.* Many promotional campaigns for banks and brokerage services show consumers receiving personalized service. The reality may be quite different—the personal banker is often busy, relatively inexperienced, and offers solutions that are prepackaged recipes; the brokerage account executive mouths the latest line from the firm's research department—nothing very personalized in either case. The problem is basic economics: When dealing with small family accounts, the bank or brokerage firm cannot hire the kinds of people that *could* make a difference at a price the customer can afford.

☐ *Automobiles.* Promotions by auto companies and repair services often portray craftsmen taking the time to analyze your car's problems, explaining these problems to you and then fixing them satisfactorily, in short, just the kind of person everyone would like to have working on *their* car. However, the reality is usually untrained or unskilled mechanics, repeated trips, shoddy work, misdiagnosis or no diagnosis of the problem, and so on. How can the customer help but feel gypped?

☐ *Restaurants.* Seasoned diners know that the more elaborate the prose used in the menu, the higher the probability that the reality will be abysmal. When we see an item described as "fresh spring potatoes gently fried in pure virgin olive oil and lovingly seasoned with 15 rare spices. . . ," we brace ourselves for soggy cottage fries that have been microwaved an hour earlier and will set us back a sizable sum.

### They Oversell

This goes hand-in-hand with overpromising. Generally, most companies avoid the crude bait-and-switch tactics of the past, but all too often there's considerable overpromising at the point of sale. While endemic in many areas of retailing—automobiles, appliances, some real estate transactions—occasionally industrial firms will also succumb to the temptation. Burroughs's experience with its B-800 series of computers, described in Chapter 7, is a classic example of the problems created by overselling. Several small business customers of Burroughs sued the company, claiming they had not received what they'd been promised at the time of purchase, namely, a computer system that suited their needs and that had customized software provided at a minimal cost.

### They Try To Manipulate Expectations

Some firms try to manipulate customers by using terms that may be misleading, by using pricing schemes that don't tell the whole story, or through other means. Car rental firms, for example, use the terms "subcompact," "compact," "midsized," and "luxury" in ways that, to the customer, often appear either arbitrary or downright confusing. In other cases, firms may try to convince the customer that their (valid) expectations are completely unrealistic; for example, "the software is so user-friendly that *most* users don't need any support."

### They Conceal Bad News

Airlines frequently stonewall if a flight is late, to prevent passengers from defecting to competing flights. Car rental firms hide the costs of collision damage and other insurance by making them separate charges *in addition* to their daily rates; further, they may use language that (intentionally or not) may intimidate customers into taking unnecessary coverage. Hotels in Europe are known for adding stiff handling charges for long-distance telephone calls without notifying customers in advance. The result can be a huge bill, long faces, and much uproar as unwary customers and hoteliers argue the toss. Some U.S. hotels are adopting these practices following the deregulation of the telephone industry in 1984. They "force" customers to use the hotel's long-distance company, charge the maximum (the operator-dialed rate), and quietly pocket the difference.

The end result of such tactics is that customers become cynical and the firm loses its most valuable asset—its franchise with its customers, that natural feeling of loyalty to and identification with the firm and its products that produces consistent, long-term profits, and protection from competition. Customers start automatically discounting the firm's claims to better performance, higher quality, better value, and so forth; they assume that it is just more of the same.

## WHY THESE PROBLEMS OCCUR

Firms mismanage customer expectations this way because they misunderstand, misinterpret, or ignore customer's wishes and needs; because they fail to understand the importance of atmospherics, incentives, and attitudes; because they're concentrating on getting customers to buy what they make rather than giving them what they want; because of internal pressures and incentives; or because they believe their own hype.

☐ *They Misunderstand Customer Expectations.* A frequent problem is that firms focus on the needs of the average customer and make no allowance for the potentially wide variations in how individual customers use their products. Yet these variations can be substantial; in such cases designing for the average user may leave a sizable number of customers— who are more demanding—stranded. Companies also forget that needs may not be substitutable; customers, they seem to feel, will put up with shortcomings in key areas if the price is right. Maybe so, but in many cases the dissatisfaction will remain long after the lower price is forgotten.

☐ *They Don't Understand How Atmospherics Affect Expectations.* While companies go to great lengths to control the content of their advertising, they often pay much less attention to the atmospherics—the conditions under which the customer is directly exposed to their products before and during the sale. It is useless for an airline to invite close inspection with an expensive and slick advertising campaign if the reception areas are dirty, the planes themselves are congested, connection information is difficult to obtain, and so forth. While some of these deficiencies relate to performance, they're also part and parcel of the atmospherics—in the customer's eyes, they project what the firm really is, while the advertising projects how the firm would like to be. Similarly, the impact of an auto repair service promotion is lost if potential customers are kept waiting on the service phone, the service receptionist has a harassed or bored attitude, the technicians are not well-dressed or use profanity in front of waiting customers, and so forth.

☐ *They Force-Fit Expectations to Internal Capabilities.* A very common mistake is to give customers what you can produce, rather than what they really want, and then use pricing or other considerations to compensate for the dissatisfaction. A classic example is the auto industry practice of bundling options—forcing customers to purchase needless (but profitable) options in order to get a feature they really want, (e.g., performance packages that come with needless extras, when the customer merely wants a stiffer suspension, trim packages, and so forth). The assumption here is that, for the right price, customers will stretch, or adjust, their needs to suit the company's production capabilities. Perhaps so, but they won't be satisfied and their expectations about the company's products will reflect this—"They do the job, but aren't as convenient—buy 'em if the price is right!"

☐ *They Succumb to Internal Pressures and Disregard the Impact on Expectations.* Airlines behave in a fashion that, in many cases, seriously undermines the expectations created by expensive advertising campaigns. They often don't provide passengers with timely information regarding delays; they hold the planes on the ground and sometimes cancel flights that may not be very full in order to consolidate loads; some avoid serving meals at all costs, and so forth. Similarly, banks virtually force customers to use automated tellers in order to reduce their own labor costs, ignoring what this does to their advertising campaign that seeks to make the bank appear friendlier to the customer—personal banking done with a teller that beeps and squeaks.

☐ *They Confuse Expectations with Advertising.*  At times it seems that companies view customers as having no memories other than those created by the firm's advertising. Only this can explain U.S. automakers' frustration with consumers for not accepting at face value their claims that quality has improved.

The underlying cause, of course, is the cost-oriented focus. Creating the right set of expectations and meeting them satisfactorily takes time and money—lots of it. Most managements prefer to do it inexpensively; they convince themselves that a snappy advertising campaign, coupled with a few short-term programs, will cure any problems with quality, reliability, or performance. However, the consumer is rarely fooled—almost never, in the long run. Thus the effect of these tactics is the very opposite of what management wanted: Buyers become more cynical, they have lower expectations, and, in a competitive market, they will buy only if the price is right—which means lower than that charged by firms whose products provide greater satisfaction.

## WHAT THE WINNERS DO

The firms in our survey took great pains to understand and manage their customers' expectations. They took care to ensure that their actions created only those expectations the firm could meet. They were conscious of the impact of atmospherics, attitudes, and incentives and concentrated considerable attention on these areas. They communicated extensively with their customers, alerting them to problems before they occurred and modifying customers' expectations as appropriate, thereby preventing needless disappointments. In addition, a very important ingredient is the emphasis our winners gave to meeting customer commitments almost regardless of expense.

### They're Careful about the Expectations They Create

Federal Express is the prime example: The focus is on "absolutely, positively" overnight 10:30 A.M. The message is very direct, with no "provideds" or other qualifying clauses. Federal Express says that if they pick up your package by a certain time, it will reach its destination by 10:30 the next morning, or else you get your money back. Contrast this with the U.S. Postal Service's Express Mail service, where there are so many caveats that the user isn't clear exactly what is being offered—delivery by 10:30 or 4:30, do they deliver or does the package have to be picked up, how do I get my money back if it's late, and so forth. Mercedes-Benz carefully stresses quality and engineering, not luxury, in its advertising, in promotional literature, and in all communications. Maytag's lonely repairman projects an image of high reliability; however, nowhere does he (or Maytag) claim that Maytag appliances never fail. Northwestern Mutual stresses the fact that it is the "quiet company" whose agents *listen* to their customers' needs and concerns.

Particularly worth noting was the fact that (1) their message was simple, easy to understand, and not cluttered with other themes, and (2) it was very consistent with their overall focus and corporate strategy. Federal Express stresses "absolutely, positively" and gears its entire system to deliver to that expectation. They don't mention price, or try to compare themselves with competitors or whatever. The main, and possibly only, expectation Federal Express wants to create is that of absolute credibility in its ability to deliver your packages overnight, by 10:30 in the morning. Maytag is stressing premium quality and reliability through its design, advertising, engineering, pricing, and theme of the lonely repairman. It doesn't confuse its message by talking about sales opportunities, coupons, or other gimmicks. Century 21 Real Estate Corporation's advertising programs are consistent with their theme of superior satisfaction; they don't mention price or promotions or multiple features, merely good people, working for a good firm, and providing superior customer satisfaction.

### They Control Atmospherics, Attitudes, and Incentives Carefully

Mercedes-Benz's Signature Service™ is a structured program designed to ensure that its dealers provide Mercedes-Benz customers with superior service support. Their goal is to "provide service unparalleled in industry"; if the percentage of owners who continue to use the dealer's service department is any guide, Mercedes-Benz has succeeded. In the mid-1970s, Deere carried out a major overhaul of its dealers' facilities. Deere encouraged its dealers to build fresh new facilities. Then once the dealer was committed to a new building, Deere provided architectural and design assistance to make certain that the new building would be consistent with the Deere image. This assistance went into every area of dealership operations, from the uniforms service technicians should wear (yellow and green, Deere colors) to the layout of the parts counter and the arrangement of the merchandise on the showroom floor. Federal Express uses graphics, uniforms, and packaging to promote a consistent image of quality, reliability, and performance—very different from the earlier delivery boy image prevalent in the industry. Northwestern Mutual recruits and trains high-quality agents to maintain a pinstripe image. If the agent wants to advertise locally, his or her message must be cleared through the home office. Agents are prohibited from giving legal advice to policyowners, and there is specific language in their sales proposals emphasizing that dividends are not guaranteed. CENTURY 21's gold jackets for their real estate agents are a visual symbol of what house buyers can expect when they walk into a Century 21 office.

Nor is this attention to detail restricted to atmospherics or external packaging alone. These companies pay considerable attention to the attitudes and incentives of their salesforce and their intermediaries to ensure that they are consistent with the image the firm wishes to create in the customers' minds. Century 21 Real Estate Corporation developed training programs to move a real estate salesperson away from only selling physical property and toward a better understanding of the motivations, as well as the trauma inherent in any move. The firm's goal was to change the real estate salesperson's focus from earning commissions to serving client needs.

### They Communicate Extensively with the Customer

In its restaurant food distribution operations, Kraft calls ahead if they do not have a particular item. This allows the restaurant operator to substitute menu items, change recipes, or locate other sources in time. Xerox service personnel call ahead to let the customer know when they will be coming out to fix the machine. This removes the uncertainty in customers' minds; it also allows them to determine the seriousness of the problem in advance of the service person's visit. Further, service technicians are encouraged to make follow-up telephone calls to find out if any problems remain and generally to increase customers' comfort level.

Companies' reasons for such extensive communication with the customer are twofold. First, they want to show that they're anticipating and working around problems, rather than reacting, or worse yet, covering up. This strengthens their credibility with customers, thereby ensuring that buyers will believe any promises or commitments the company makes. Second, they want to learn about and, where possible, modify any expectations the customer has that the company will be unable to meet. By alerting customers early about potential problems and creating a joint problem-solving approach to the situation, these firms ensure that customers' expectations will not be so high as to guarantee unhappiness. For example, a restaurant that does business with Kraft Foodservice can log-in to the KRAFTLINK™ computer system early in the morning and it will see exactly what was on its invoice and what is in the Kraft truck scheduled to arrive later in the day. If the restaurant finds out that it is going to be short some items (for example, Heinz ketchup), then it still has an opportunity to go somewhere else and get it, as opposed to finding out when the truck arrives at 2:00 P.M., and it's two hours away from starting dinner preparations without a vital ingredient.

### They Emphasize Meeting Commitments to Customers Almost Regardless of Cost

This is key to the companies' success in managing customers' expectations. Buyers know that the firm *will* deliver what it has promised, when it has promised, and at the price it has promised. Thus it is no coincidence that every one of our winners continually stresses the importance of meeting commitments to customers. They do this in training of sales and service personnel, in the rewards and incentives they provide/suggest to their channels, and in their corporate values by the recognition given to outstanding performers, the folklore of the firm, and so forth. This emphasis communicates itself to their customers and strengthens their confidence in the firm.

## A SOUND FOUNDATION

Many firms believe that providing a good, well-designed product is enough to keep customers happy. While a good product is essential for high customer satisfaction, by itself it is not enough.

Companies must learn how to understand and control—not manipulate—customers' needs so that buyers (1) understand what they are receiving, (2) are able to relate the product to their needs, and (3) convince themselves that it is completely satisfactory. If this doesn't occur, customers' satisfaction with the product will, at best, be temporary. Sooner or later buyers are going to realize that the product doesn't meet important needs and will feel disappointed, sometimes even gypped. Therefore companies must be careful to create the right expectations or else face the consequences.

# 7

## *Intermediaries*

### *AMBASSADORS OR ASSASSINS?*

The vast majority of products and services are sold through third-party intermediaries—distributors, dealers, franchises, merchandisers, department stores, retail outlets, supermarkets, and so forth. These intermediaries (or channels or dealers—we will use the three terms interchangeably) are a vital link between a firm and its customers. Ideally, the intermediary should act as an ambassador for the firm it represents. It should be an envoy, representing the company and its products in the best possible way to its customers, working to ensure maximum customer satisfaction and continued friendly relations between the customer and the company.

Frequently, however, the customer believes that the intermediary, like an ambassador, is someone "who lies abroad for the good of his or her country" (or company). Customers may distrust the information provided by the dealer, viewing it as company-sponsored propaganda. They may believe that the dealer, rather than adding value to the product or service, merely adds cost—and therefore raises the price. Consumer Reports, for example, suggests that an auto dealer should be restricted to a price between $200 and $400 above the dealer's cost for the car and any options. Consequently, buyers of many products—cars, clothing, appliances, and televisions, to name a few—may seek to bypass the chosen channel in purchases, in after-sales support, and in complaint handling and problem resolution.

Many companies, in their turn, treat channels as necessary nuisances. They bypass them regularly in communicating with the customer. They increase the number of channels, thereby reducing each channel's profitability. They change channels frequently. In short, they do their best to make the intermediaries irrelevant, where they cannot eliminate them altogether.

As a result, the ambassador starts behaving more and more like a poorly paid assassin who takes on any and all assignments. Dealers represent just about any firm, without inquiring too closely into products or credentials. They abandon products rapidly, leaving customers stranded. They skimp on marketing and support, preferring to hustle, or rush, customers into a sale—any sale—and abandoning them immediately afterward.

The bottom line is a mugging of the customer, the dealer, and ultimately the company. In the long run, nobody wins. Customers are not satisfied with their products, companies with their intermediaries, or intermediaries with their customers or their companies.

Intermediaries can make or break a firm's efforts to establish a franchise with its customers and are thus a critical element in ensuring overall customer satisfaction. Specifically, our research indicates the following:

□ *Satisfaction with the Dealer and Overall Satisfaction Go Hand-in-Hand*. If customers are happy with the dealer, they will likely be happy with the product. Conversely, dissatisfaction with the intermediary rubs off on the product as well.

□ *Dealers Determine Customers' Attitudes and Expectations*. Dealers do this directly through their actions (e.g., advertising, in-store communications, salespeople's attitudes, pricing, packaging, etc.). They also do it indirectly through their attitudes about the customer and the manufacturer (e.g., sales incentives, organization, and profit measurements).

□ *Dealers Affect Product Performance*. This is self-evident for service businesses (e.g., fast food, real estate), where the dealer manufactures the service. It is also true for tangible goods, especially in cases where after-sales support is important.

□ *Dealers Influence Customer Feedback and Restitution*. By acting as filters for complaints, dealers can affect customer satisfaction, sometimes drastically.

Although these conclusions may appear obvious, many firms and industries appear to be oblivious to the damage their intermediaries cause. Airlines and airports provide a case in point. Airports act as an intermediary for the airlines, delivering and receiving millions of customers each year. Yet at most airports the prices of goods—coffee, gum, a doughnut, candy or a snack—are nothing short of outrageous. When we pointed this out to a senior airline executive, the response was, "It's totally outrageous. But we can't do anything about it. The airports set their own prices . . . and in most cases they're out to get all they can." He shouldn't be surprised, therefore, when passengers entering his airplane are grouchy and resentful; maybe they've just paid 85 cents for a small cup of weak coffee. More important, unable to express their anger at the airport, they're likely to vent their frustrations on the airline.

## SATISFACTION WITH THE DEALER AFFECTS OVERALL SATISFACTION

The level of customer satisfaction with the intermediary has a great deal to do with overall customer satisfaction. A strong dealer network that concentrates on keeping customers happy increases their satisfaction with almost any product. Conversely, an indifferent or downright poor intermediary drags down satisfaction levels for even the best products. For example, when customers have a problem, their natural response is to blame the manufacturer, even for things that are the dealer's fault. David Berliner of Consumers Union thinks, "It's the issue of people not knowing whom to blame [when it's the dealer's fault]. It really narrows down to frustration. And it rebounds to the nonbenefit, if you will, of the manufacturer, because ultimately it's the manufacturer to whom people will look. They have a product and on it is the name General Electric, or Whirlpool, or anyone."

Research done in the automotive industry has established the close connection between customer satisfaction with the dealer and overall satisfaction. Since 1980, J.D. Power & Associates, a major market research firm, has polled more than 60,000 car owners in the United States to measure their satisfaction with product quality and dealer service during the first 12 to 14 months of ownership. The annual survey covers every major make of domestic, Japanese and European cars sold in the United States during the preceding year. Respondents are asked to evaluate their car purchase on a number of factors, such as delivery conditions, the attitude and behavior of the dealership service advisor, the standards of service provided, their overall evaluation of the dealership service department, and parts availability. In addition, the participants are asked:

If they would purchase the same make again,

If they would purchase their next car from the same dealer, and

How they would rate their overall satisfaction with their car.

Upon analyzing the survey results, we see at once the pervasive impact of satisfaction with the dealer on overall customer satisfaction.

☐ *Overall Customer Satisfaction and Satisfaction with the Dealer Track Very Closely.* As Figure 7.1 shows, the more satisfied customers were with the dealership, the greater was their overall satisfaction with their cars, and vice versa. Rarely, if ever, were customers very satisfied with their car while being dissatisfied with the dealer. There was little or no difference between domestic cars and most imports when it came to satisfaction with the dealer; thus the much greater level of overall customer satisfaction with imports was due primarily to the product itself.

☐ *High Satisfaction with the Dealer Plus High Product Quality Equals a Winner.* Mercedes-Benz, Subaru, and Jaguar lead the other makes in customer satisfaction with the dealer. When combined with their overall high-product quality, this proved to be an unbeatable combination.

☐ *Satisfaction with the Dealer Leads to Greater Loyalty to the Dealer.* (See Figure 7.2.) When customers are satisfied with a dealership, they're more likely to purchase their next car from the same dealership. Customers who were most satisfied with their dealerships showed a nearly 25 percent higher intention of purchasing their next car from the same dealer.

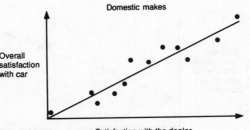

*Figure 7.1 Overall customer satisfaction and satisfaction with the dealer track very closely*

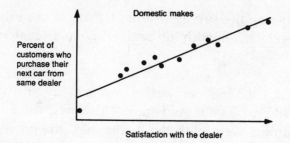

*Figure 7.2 Satisfaction with the dealer leads to greater loyalty to the dealer*

☐ *Satisfaction with the Dealer Leads to Greater Brand Loyalty*. The happier customers are with the dealership, the greater the probability that they will purchase the same make again (see Figure 7.3).

The situation is the same in other industries, such as farm equipment, construction machinery, and general aviation: Customer satisfaction with the product is inextricably linked to customer satisfaction with the dealer. To the customer, the intermediary *is* the manufacturer. The dealer is the only point at which the vast majority of customers have first-hand contact with the manufacturer.

Given that we can measure customer satisfaction as the difference between perceived performance and expectations (see Chapter 2), the major role that satisfaction with the dealer plays in overall satisfaction becomes understandable. Intermediaries affect customer

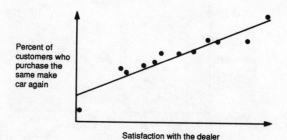

*Figure 7.3 Satisfaction with the dealer leads to greater brand loyalty*

expectations by reinforcing or distorting the messages sent by the manufacturer. Intermediaries affect perceived performance by how, and how well, they provide after-sales support and handle customer complaints or problems. Finally, intermediaries affect the manufacturer's reactions to changes in customer needs or product-related problems.

## DEALERS AFFECT CUSTOMER EXPECTATIONS

Consumers of every product or service have expectations regarding its performance, durability, utility, value, and so on. Manufacturers spend billions of dollars in design, packaging, advertising, and promotion to send the right messages to potential customers. Intermediaries modulate this message—reinforce it or distort it—directly through their own messages and actions, and indirectly through their attitudes about the customers they serve, the manufacturers they represent, and their own role in the entire value chain.

1. *Directly.* Channels affect the manufacturer's message through the location, external appearance, layout, and user-friendliness of their facilities; the attitudes, appearance, and product knowledge of their sales and service personnel; the type of sales approach they use (hard sell versus soft sell, consultative or confrontational); the overt and covert messages and the quality of their advertising and promotion; the presence or absence of bait and switch tactics; and the degree of flexibility in their pricing policies.

All of these factors, in combination, have a dramatic impact on the customers' expectations and, therefore, on the level of likely postpurchase satisfaction with the product or service.

Burroughs Corporation's experiences with its B-800 minicomputer provide an interesting case study of how false expectations created by dealers and sales personnel can create extensive—and expensive—problems. In 1980, the following advertisement appeared in the *Wall Street Journal*:

> Attention: Unhappy users of Burroughs B-800 and similar Burroughs computer hardware and software. Our firm is preparing to sue the Burroughs Corporation. We would like to find other firms who, like us, feel that overly zealous computer salespeople may have misrepresented the Burroughs B-800 or similar product lines to them. We wish to combine our information in efforts to seek a solution to our problems using all available legal remedies. All responses will be treated confidentially.

This advertisement was placed by a disgruntled purchaser of a Burroughs B-800, a small distribution company that was suing Burroughs for failure to deliver what had been promised and, so the owner claimed, almost bankrupting the firm in the process. It generated 350 responses from other dissatisfied B-800 owners with similar problems and created a major embarrassment for Burroughs. Most of these customers had been assured that the B-800 would be adequate for their needs', company sales personnel and/or dealers had promised that Burroughs would develop and customize necessary software. They had also promised that these software changes would be either free or made at a nominal charge and would be available quickly.

What actually happened was that, for many customers, the capacity of the B-800 was barely adequate. Furthermore the promised modifications were slow in coming and raised the cost of the system considerably. To top it all, in some cases the software didn't do the job, or did it inadequately. Ultimately, Burroughs settled with a number of these customers for an undisclosed (but presumably large) sum.

All the winners we interviewed are fully aware of this modulation by the channel and work to ensure that the channel's efforts are directed toward reinforcing the company's messages. Deere's efforts with its dealerships provide one of the best examples of how successful companies effect this reinforcement. Throughout the 1970s, Deere gently insisted that its dealers rebuild or remodel their facilities. Once the dealers agreed, they received guidance on the size of the building, the layout of the parking lot and display areas, the placement of merchandise on the floor, and so on. Deere suggested that dealership personnel be given uniforms. The company encouraged the dealers to use standardized fixtures and amenities (e.g., Enter and Exit signs on the driveway with the Deere logo) that the company provided. The result is that when customers drive up to the dealership along a well-landscaped, clearly marked driveway they notice a high-quality image. As they enter the store, they see an attractive floor display and are greeted by neatly dressed sales and counter personnel. The service area is clean and well-lighted, with no mess and no idle employees. In short, customers are reassured that wherever they go, they will receive Deere quality and Deere support.

2. *Indirectly.* Intermediaries' attitudes about the customer, the manufacturer, and ultimately themselves have at least as great an effect on customers' expectations as do the intermediaries' direct actions. Consciously and subconsciously, customers receive signals that alert them to the intermediary's true feelings. If these hidden signals are inconsistent with the overt messages—if the advertising pitch stresses value and the salesperson emphasizes price—customers are confused.

To many people, their physician's intermediaries, such as nurses, doctor's receptionists, assistants, and hospital staff, appear to view the patient as a necessary evil to be dealt with as quickly as possible. This attitude manifests itself in many ways: overscheduling of patients, long waiting times, demands for immediate payment, and unwillingness to deal with an individual insurance company's reporting requirements. If a patient appears impatient, fidgets, or complains, he or she is told, "The doctor's rather busy right now." The implicit attitudinal message is quite simple: "The doctor's time is more valuable than your, so be patient and

wait." (The very word for customer—*patient*—is highly revealing.) The customer understands this and reacts accordingly by expressing dissatisfaction with the doctor and the medical profession as a whole.

Dealers' attitudes toward the manufacturers they represent also
affect the customer. Deere's dealers, almost without exception,
are proud to represent Deere and Co. and to be part of a successful, customer-oriented organization. Therefore, their response to
any customer problem is to try to solve it as best they can, en-
listing company support when necessary. Rarely will they pass
the buck or say, "It's Deere's policy; our hands are tied." General
aviation dealers, by and large, have the opposite attitude; they
generally have a low opinion of the various manufacturers. They
appear to live in a state of constant (if subdued) tension characterized by a high turnover of dealers, lawsuits, and mutual recrimi-
nation. This affects their attitudes toward the manufacturers and
their products, in turn affecting customer satisfaction with the
makers.

## DEALERS AFFECT PRODUCT PERFORMANCE

Intermediaries have considerable impact on the perceived and actual performance of the products and services they sell and,
therefore, on customer satisfaction. In many cases they do so directly, because they produce the overall product; examples of
such intermediaries are VARs and VADs (value-added resellers
and dealers, respectively), franchisees, and system integrators.
Others, such as equipment dealers, distributors, and mass merchandisers, affect product performance through the level and
quality of after-sales support they provide.

VARs, VADs, and franchisees affect product performance directly
through their own quality control and manufacturing capabilities.
In many cases, especially in service industries, the parent compa-

ny's role is limited to providing national advertising, training franchisee personnel, and providing key ingredients. As Bruce Oseland, senior vice president of Century 21® Real Estate Corp., puts it, "We sell a service. We don't have a product. The product we sell in our advertising is someone who wears a gold coat and the image and the service capabilities of that individual."

Intermediaries that sell packaged goods, appliances, equipment, and so on affect product performance by the way they handle customers' needs after the sale. Although the manufacturer may try to eliminate potential problems through product design, it is virtually impossible to anticipate all such problems. Consequently, the channel plays an important role in maximizing product performance through the after-sales support it provides. A Maytag washer will not provide expected levels of performance if it is not installed correctly. Similarly, a Mercedes-Benz owner will not be happy if the dealership service is sloppy. Figures 7.1 through 7.3 dramatically illustrate the impact of after-sales support on product performance and customer satisfaction. Both domestic and Japanese car manufacturers receive about the same level of support from their dealer organizations. Thus the difference in overall satisfaction is primarily related to product quality. On the other hand, Subaru, Jaguar, and Mercedes-Benz receive much greater levels of support from their dealerships, thereby boosting perceived product performance and satisfaction.

## DEALERS AFFECT FEEDBACK

Intermediaries are also a feedback loop, sending information from the customer to the manufacturer. In this role they help to determine (1) the quality and quantity of the feedback the manufacturer receives, (2) how quickly the manufacturer responds to this feedback, and (3) how well the manufacturer performs in the interim, while the problem is being corrected.

☐ *Quality and Quantity of Feedback.* Customers' reactions to a product are a mixture of signal (information about real problems, design deficiencies, and performance constraints) combined with noise (complaints about problems that arise because of willful misuse, neglect, ignorance, or operator carelessness). Channels can act as either filters, blockers, or amplifiers of these reactions. A good channel will act as an effective filter, separating and forwarding the important messages to the manufacturer, while dealing with the trivial on its own initiative. Indifferent or poor intermediaries often block the signal, perhaps believing that the company would disregard it, thus forcing the manufacturer to seek other ways of obtaining feedback. Or worse yet, they act as amplifiers, blaming all problems, including those created by their own shortcomings, on the manufacturer.

☐ *Speed of Response.* Channels heavily influence the speed with which a manufacturer responds, or, perhaps more important, is perceived by customers to respond, to problems. This is a function of the intermediaries' clout with the manufacturer and of the manufacturer's views and attitudes toward the intermediary.

☐ *Interim Performance.* Every firm has its share of product problems. Channels have a great impact on how well the manufacturer fares in the interim between discovering the problem and fixing it. A good intermediary will help the manufacturer maintain its market share or at least lose as little of it as possible; indifferent or poor intermediaries may turn a potentially minor problem into a sometimes fatal disaster.

Deere's experiences with its 8430/8630 line of four-wheel-drive tractors illustrate how channels affect feedback. Introduced in 1974, these machines, costing about $60,000 each, represented Deere's rather belated entry into a fast-growing market. Initially, these machines had problems in major areas, a consequence perhaps of their being moved too rapidly into production to meet competitive pressures. Their engines failed frequently, there were performance and design problems with their transmissions, and the hydraulics had glitches in them. In mid-1975, Deere had a potential disaster on its hands.

The dealers' reactions to this crisis were highly instructive. First, key dealers helped the company separate the signal from the noise. One West Coast dealer, for example, prepared a detailed, well-documented presentation, replete with statistics that summarized key problem areas and suggested priorities. Next, the strong relationship between the dealers and Deere ensured that company management responded rapidly and effectively to the problems. Deere recognized that it faced a crisis and reacted swiftly by redesigning components and subsystems that failed frequently, changing manufacturing processes, and issuing retrofits. Finally, the dealers ensured that farmers stayed loyal to Deere throughout this period. Essentially, they said to the customer, "We know they've had some problems, but don't worry about it. I'm here and Deere's here to stand behind the equipment and fix it, regardless." As a result, Deere captured and maintained a respectable share of the four-wheel-drive market despite its late start.

## THE VIRTUOUS CIRCLE

All the companies we interviewed recognize the power of intermediaries in maximizing customer satisfaction and have invested substantially in time, money, and people to build strong channel relations. These companies have recognized the power of what we will term the "virtuous circle" that links product, customer satisfaction, customer demand, channel profits, and company profits. Karl Faber of Mercedes-Benz explained that a good product results in high demand, which produces a healthy and profitable dealer organization, which allows Mercedes-Benz to demand that dealers invest in the company, which results in a good product. This theme was repeated in company after company.

- ☐ At Jaguar, chairman and chief executive, John Egan, called it the "customer satisfaction cycle." Key to Jaguar's turnaround, in his opinion, was the discovery that "if we could only make the cars work, they would sell." As soon as Jaguar was able to convince the dealers that the cars did indeed work, sales came roaring back.
- ☐ Fred Maytag II recognized that "to be successful you've got to serve the interest of the shareholders, dealers, customers, and employees. . . . Unless in the long term you serve the needs of all those people, your company will not be successful."
- ☐ Northwestern Mutual calls it the "circle of success": The company provides a product with high value. The opportunity to sell this high-value product attracts better agents. These agents sell to upscale, well-informed customers, which in turn increases the value of the company.

This virtuous circle can also work in reverse, with a vengeance: A poor product may attract less well-informed and less loyal customers, which reduces the profitability of the dealer. In turn, the dealer is then less willing to invest in the company's product, which further reduces demand, which further reduces profit, and so forth. There are many examples: AMC/Renault, Fiat, and British Leyland in automobiles; International Harvester in farm equipment, trucks, and industrial equipment; Commodore in home computers.

The virtuous circle has benefits both near- and long-term. In the near term, it can act like a turbo charger, providing a quick boost to increase or maintain sales, lift share, or generally pick up momentum. Long term, the virtuous circle creates a major strategic barrier for other competitors and new entrants.

### Turbo Charger

Jaguar's experience provides perhaps the most graphic illustration of the boost such a virtuous circle can provide. In 1980, Jaguar sold barely 3000 cars in North America, and the company was flat on its back. In 1985, more than 24,000 Jaguars were sold in the United States alone, and the firm is now soaring. The key to its success was the fact that management concentrated on getting a reliable product to a strong dealer organization. It let dealers know that it was aware of the car's problems, kept them informed about progress, and met its commitments to the dealers on time. The effect was dramatic. According to John Egan, "at the tail end of 1980 [I went] over to the United States and I met all of the dealers and I gave them the strangest sales presentation. What I did do [was] to tell them about our quality program, and in which month their favorite complaints would be solved." He compared it to a revival meeting: "Gentlemen, on the first of January [1981], Jaguar introduces its North American dealers to the round tire, and there were roars of approval. Then I said, 'In February, the radio aerial will go up and will go down.' Another roar of approval. By the time I was finished, they said, 'If you can make cars without problems, we can break all records.' Later on, I said I was disappointed with the North American dealers who only wanted to go to 6000 cars [in 1981], and one chap stood up and said, 'I stand for the Southern California dealers and we will double sales.' And other people said they would double sales. At just this time we brought in the Grenadier Guards' [big roaring] band, and I said, 'Is it 9000?' And they said 'Yes!!' We actually sold 10,000 cars." By 1985 Jaguar's sales had soared to 20,528 in the United States alone.

### Strategic Resources

In the long term, this close-knit relationship between product quality, customer satisfaction, dealer profitability, and company success can, if managed carefully, become a formidable strategic resource. A well-run, well-organized network of intermediaries, when coupled with products that are geared toward high customer satisfaction, provides several long-term competitive advantages:

☐ *It Deters New Entrants.* The virtuous circle raises the stakes for any new entrant—domestic or import—considerably. Just ask Komatsu how it has fared against Caterpillar in the United States market. Not very well at all!

☐ *It Provides Timely Feedback.* Close links with intermediaries enable manufacturers to learn quickly about shifts in customers' needs, competitive positioning, pricing threats, and so on.

☐ *It Smooths Out "Stumbles."* New product introductions and model changeovers are always fraught with risk. The virtuous circle takes out much of the risk by providing an early warning for problems, and working to contain and minimize the potential damage caused by introductory glitches, as illustrated by Deere's experiences with its 8430/8630 line of tractors, discussed previously.

☐ *It Stretches Product Life.* Strong intermediaries can reduce the need for frequent changes, provided the basic design provides high customer satisfaction. Apple Computer's strong support of its dealer network has helped prolong the life of the Apple II microcomputer, a prehistoric model by microcomputer standards.

## HOW THE WINNERS DO IT

Upon analyzing how the winners created the virtuous circle, we identified four common characteristics.

☐ *They Select Intermediaries with Great Care.* All the companies were very careful in deciding which channels to use and whom to have represent them within each type of channel.

☐ *They Work Hard to Make the Channel Succeed*. The profitability of these companies' channels was consistently above average, in large measure because the parent firm worked hard at producing this profitability.

☐ *They Set and Enforce High Standards for Their Intermediaries*. These companies did not roll over and surrender to their channels. On the contrary, they enforced stringent performance demands.

☐ *They Build Long-Term Relationships with Their Intermediaries*. Their turnover of dealers was lower than that of their competitors.

### Select Intermediaries Carefully

Many firms appear to be willing to allow just about anybody to represent them and their products; their focus appears to be more geographic than anything else. In marketing terms, they view intermediaries as so many points on a map and are more concerned about having empty locations (areas without representation) than they are about who represents them in each location. For example: Throughout much of the 1960s and 1970s, virtually all it took to be a general aviation dealer was a love of flying, access to an airfield, and perhaps $2000 in cash. The manufacturers were more than willing to advance liberal credit terms and provide new aircraft as long as the dealer sold his or her quota. As a result, general aviation dealerships mushroomed, with high turnover and many failures.

By contrast, the firms we interviewed chose their intermediaries with great care. Nunn explained that Maytag, for example, "will not franchise a dealer unless there is assurance of customer service either through that dealer's own service department or through a servicing organization that Maytag approves . . . [they]

want to be 100 percent sure that any customer who buys a Maytag has the assurance of service in the event service is required."

Deere and Caterpillar require potential dealers to have adequate financial resources and staying power; this ranges from a net worth of $500,000 to over $5 million. Northwestern Mutual looks for agents with a high-quality, businesslike image.

In all of these cases, the priority appears to be more on the person or organization that would represent the manufacturer and less on coverage of a specific location. To quote Boyd Bartlett, president of Deere, "I knew that my father's balance sheet wasn't that strong, but he was about 40 years old at the time and I think they saw him as a guy with the determination to make it and expand." Maytag's Nunn puts it similarly, "In developing a dealer organization, we look for a quality retailer just as we do in looking for quality people to work for our company. We want a dealer who runs a good business, who's well-organized, who has competent salespeople and who is financially capable of operating a successful business." Nunn's observation is key: *Winners want to be certain that the intermediary who will represent them is as good as any of their own people.* In all these firms, the fundamental question appears to be, "Is this the person we want representing us to our customers?" The emphasis seems to be as much qualitative as quantitative, as much on that intangible fit as on tangibles such as net worth, education, prior experience, and location.

### Make Intermediaries Succeed

These companies don't stop at intermediary selection; they work hard to make the intermediary succeed. And make no mistake about it, these companies' dealers are successful.

☐ McDonald's has no shortage of applicants for its franchises, despite high capital requirements; clearly there's money to be made in a McDonald's franchise.

☐ In the 1970s, Deere dealers averaged over 25.6 percent on their net worth, far in excess of the industry average of 18.6 percent. They have also weathered the prolonged slump in farm equipment sales far better than any of their competitors.

☐ Northwestern Mutual has a higher proportion of its agents in the Million Dollar Roundtable than other top companies (25 percent vs. the 4 percent average for the top 20 companies), and in Chartered Life Underwriters (35 percent vs. 6 percent); 32 percent of them have also received National Quality Awards.

The pattern is the same in automobiles and in appliances: The intermediaries of the winners are much more successful financially than are their counterparts who represent other firms.

Our research shows that these results are not accidental. On the contrary, they're tangible proof to the intermediary of the value of being part of the virtuous circle, and these results occur because the firms work hard at making them happen.

*Why Do These Firms Do It?* All of these companies are keenly aware of the importance of practically guaranteeing their dealers' success. Their reasons are not hard to understand.

☐ It builds up the value of the franchise, which makes it easier to attract and retain high-quality channels and channel members.

☐ It ensures loyalty and support for company programs, especially for those longer-term investments that, from the channel's perspective, offer little or no immediate returns.

☐ It keeps the initiative with the manufacturers as opposed to the channel; the manufacturer controls the channel, not vice versa.

***How Do They Do It?*** The major vehicle is education. The winners provide their dealers with extensive training in all areas: product, technical, managerial, accounting, and financial. Caterpillar even runs a school for its dealers' children, helping them to enter the family business. These training programs are set apart from those of other companies by their breadth and their depth: They concentrate on every aspect of channel operations. The efforts of Century 21 Real Estate Corporation are typical. The company realized that existing real estate training was overly technical. So Century 21® started developing programs to shift the focus from selling physical property "to better understanding the motivation . . . the trauma, that's inherent in any move like the feeling that, 'I don't mind leaving Huntington Beach and moving to Chicago, if only I could take that house and set it down in a neighborhood in Chicago.' "

A major and sometimes hidden purpose of these training programs is to help inculcate the values and beliefs of the parent company in the franchisees. Bruce Oseland, of Century 21®, said, "The goal is to get [the franchisees] thinking more about, 'If I serve my client's needs in the manner in which I've been trained to do, the money will come,' as opposed to 'If I sell that house, I get $4000 commission from it.' "

The training programs are backed by company support systems in all areas, such as market analyses, sales aids, dealership design, sales personnel selection, financial analysis, financial performance comparison, and computerization. For example, Deere has separate company personnel calling on the dealer to provide assistance in analyzing service problems, merchandising and ordering parts, reviewing financial statements, training the dealership bookkeeper or accountant, and so on; nearly three company personnel support the dealer for every one soliciting orders. These company personnel are backed in turn by corporate support systems, usually computerized—for example, the DPARTS system for ordering parts, the FLASH system for placing emergency orders, and the dealer Financial Information System for keeping financial control. Northwestern Mutual has Life Insurance Network (LINK), a computer network that connects its 112 general agencies to the home office. Agents tie in to this network with personal computers and have immediate access to policyowners' records, updates, messages, and customer proposals.

Other firms provide similar support to their intermediaries without creating the same synergy. What sets the winners apart are two intangibles: *self-discipline* in their dealings with the channel and *friendly persuasion* in their approach to any changes.

1. *Self-Discipline.* The companies we interviewed try to ensure that their intermediaries view the relationship as mutually beneficial, as something in which both sides win. To make certain that this happens, these companies go to great lengths to avoid doing anything that might be viewed as exploiting their dealers. They refrain from loading the dealers with excessive inventories, even if that means cutting back their own production. They carefully balance the size of each intermediary's market area to ensure that there is adequate sales potential. They monitor intermediary profits to ensure that their channels remain financially viable. They provide financial assistance in one fashion or another to dealers in temporary difficulties.

A prolonged slump hit the farm equipment industry in the 1980s, with sales hovering at abysmally low levels. In 1985, total industry tractor sales were under 70,000 units, as compared with the peak of over 225,000 units reached in 1980. Two proved names—International Harvester and Allis-Chalmers—are no longer independent entities; a third, Massey-Ferguson, is reduced to a shadow of itself. Hundreds of farm equipment dealerships have been closed. Throughout this extremely trying period, Deere has retained the majority of its dealers. One industry analyst said in a *Wall Street Transcript* review of the industry in March 1983, "Deere has gone around and actually to the detriment of their balance sheet given support to their dealers. They're the only people who are going to end up with a healthy dealer network. Ten to twelve percent of the farm equipment dealers in 1982 went out of business, but the number of Deere dealers that went out of business was minuscule. . . . "

2. *Friendly Persuasion.* This is the other characteristic that sets the winners apart from the rest. They rarely browbeat or coerce their dealers or use a temporary upsurge in demand to extract concessions from them. Their entire approach is conciliatory, using persuasion and reason rather than economic muscle. Egan at Jaguar has been careful to ensure that dealers buy in to all the changes; he hasn't used the shortage of cars in relation to demand to ramrod through changes. Century 21 Real Estate Corporation requires that all proposed franchisee programs—seminars, handbooks, advertising—be reviewed and accepted by the franchisees before being implemented.

International Harvester's approach to its dealers provides, perhaps, the best example of how not to get the intermediary to change. In the 1950s and early 1960s, all the farm equipment companies tried to upgrade and trim their dealer bodies. However, according to Barbara Marsh in her book *A Corporate Tragedy* (Doubleday, 1985):

> Harvester's entire approach . . . smacked of the McCaffrey [the chairman] hard sell. Dealers resented Harvester's near insistence that they erect large new facilities to accommodate the company's postwar sales push. . . . [N]one pressured its dealers as adamantly as Harvester. [Dealers] who refused [to erect new buildings] faced likely cancellation of their dealership contracts. Some dealers went broke in the changeover, with many never quite getting over their bad feelings toward the company.

Sadly, the company repeated its mistakes of the 1950s again in the 1970s with its "X-L" program. The dealers, in fact, initiated this effort when they told International Harvester executives that "one of the biggest inhibitors to growth in the marketplace was a poor dealer." The X-L plan set specific standards that dealers had to meet in order to be designated as X-L dealers. The firm even

pulled ahead of Deere, technologically, by offering a computerized modeling tool to assist farmers. Ultimately 1500 dealers
joined the X-L group, but those who didn't make it felt left out.
"It ended up setting a caste system," one of the X-L dealers said.
"The company had sales meetings and programs with only X-L
dealers."

### Set and Enforce Standards

Although their approach is win–win, by no stretch of the imagi-
nation are the companies that we call "winners" pushovers for
their channels. On the contrary, they have firm, clear standards
to which they're deeply committed, and they enforce these standards on their intermediaries. Their goals are to maintain the virtuous circle and keep their leadership position. They will insist on
these standards regardless of the short-term costs. McDonald's
removed its Paris franchisee for its failure to comply with the
company's cleanliness requirements. The company spent a small
fortune on lawsuits and lost prime locations in the process. But to
McDonald's these costs were incidental compared with the risks it
would incur in any departure from its rigid standards. The company's motto is "Customers, cleanliness, service, and value."
Through this and other actions, McDonald's made its commitment to these values very clear to all its franchisees. Similarly,
Jaguar asked its U.K. dealers to meet warranty performance standards or pay stiff penalties; the company was willing to lose un-
satisfactory dealers rather than compromise on a crucial issue.

The reasons these companies set and enforce standards are twofold. First, they want to ensure that the firm's products and services are sold in a fashion that maximizes customer value. Second, they want to let everyone—customers, intermediaries,
employees, and shareholders—know of their commitment to
these values. At McDonald's, cleanliness is related to security for
the customer; it is the cornerstone of its success and thus nonne-
gotiable. Recently, Deere lowered its retail parts prices, to the

chagrin of its dealers, for whom parts sales are a much-needed source of profits in hard times. However, Deere recognized that high parts prices on widely available, high-volume items, such as hoses, oil filters, and belts, antagonized farmers. Therefore, the company tightened its own belt and required its dealers to follow suit in order to maintain customer value.

These standards can be categorized into three broad categories: those related to customer attitudes and expectations, those focusing on customer service and after-sales support, and those dealing with intermediary management and financial strength. Standards relating to customer expectations cover such items as facility location and appearance, the attire and attitudes of sales personnel, merchandising displays, local advertising and promotional materials, sales approaches, and messages. Service and after-sales support standards cover elements such as the speed with which customers must be serviced by counter personnel, the level of merchandise and parts inventories, the handling of stockouts, service technician training, service investments, and facilities. Last, standards dealing with intermediary management detail financial reporting requirements, suggest or specify accounting procedures, spell out capitalization requirements, and so on.

None of these standards is unique to the winners. General Motors, for example, has Mr. Goodwrench, a program similar in concept to Mercedes-Benz's Signature Service. Note, however, that in the J.D. Powers and Associates survey *at best* only 46 percent of GM customers considered themselves "very satisfied" with their dealership experience, as contrasted with almost 58 percent for Mercedes-Benz. What sets these winners apart is the stringency of these standards and the strict and uncompromising manner in which they are enforced.

☐ Caterpillar and Deere both require their dealers' sales and service personnel to be familiar with all of their training programs. This contrasts with the auto industry's Certified

Master Mechanic program, for example, where having one qualified mechanic per service stop was sufficient.

☐ Deere requires dealers' parts inventories to be high enough to fill at least 90 percent of customers' orders right away.

☐ Northwestern Mutual insists on a businesslike image and requires that all local advertising be cleared with the home office.

☐ Century 21 Real Estate Corporation requires that the broker/manager in all Century 21® offices, and a percentage of all full-time sales associates, complete minimum levels of training in management, investment, real estate sales, and customer assistance.

These and other examples confirm the same finding: Not only do these companies set high standards for themselves, but they demand and get similarly high levels of performance from their intermediaries.

### Build Long-Term Relationships

Many Deere and Caterpillar dealerships have been held by the same family for three, four, or even five generations. The turnover of Century 21® franchisees is very low. Jaguar kept most of its dealership franchisees throughout the 1970s and the turnaround of the 1980s. Winning companies appear to view their relationships with their dealers as old-fashioned marriages, made for the long haul. Contrast this with the high turnover among auto, general aviation, and computer dealerships.

The reasons for this long-term focus are not hard to determine.

☐ *It Makes Economic Sense.* As with customers, so also with the intermediary: A long-term relationship enables these firms to increase satisfaction, build repeat business, and lower marketing expenses through lower administrative, retraining, and dispute-resolution costs.

☐ *It Creates Forward Integration of Company Values.* Only a long-term relationship can enable the firm to inculcate its customer orientation and focus on customer satisfaction at the dealer level.

☐ *It Ensures Long-Term Customer Relations.* The customer sees the same consistent, reliable, and steady presence, year in and year out. This builds customer confidence in the company and encourages repeat purchases.

☐ *It Is Essential to the Success of the Virtuous Circle.* These firms recognize that the virtuous circle of product quality, customer satisfaction, customer demand, channel profit, and company investment is fragile; excessive turnover among channels and intermediaries would disrupt the circle and prevent the firm from obtaining the full benefits of its efforts.

# 8

# *The Real Sale Begins After the Sale*

In 1982, Deere talked to more than a thousand farmers—users of every make of agricultural equipment sold in North America—to find out why they purchased the brands of equipment that they were using on their farms. The results of the survey showed that after-sales support plays a critical role in farmers' decisions.

According to the survey, the quality of support was a deciding factor in brand choice, customer satisfaction, and brand loyalty. Farmers cited factors such as parts availability, service quality, convenience of dealership location, ease of maintenance, and high expected resale value to explain their brand choices. When these qualities were present, levels of satisfaction and of brand loyalty were high; when they were lacking, satisfaction was low. Farmers gave poor after-sales support as their primary reason for switching away from a brand when the time came to replace equipment.

As befits the industry leader, the survey results also showed that Deere was regarded by the vast majority of farmers as being head and shoulders above its competitors in providing superior quality, that is, dealer support, warranty terms, resale value, and other after-sales support elements. Deere consistently outpolled its closest competitors by ratios of two to one or better on each of these key attributes.

Deere has built and maintained its leadership position in the farm equipment industry over the past 30 years by providing good, well-designed products and backing them up by a superb after-sales support organization. It has created a strong, well-financed dealer network that has endured through the booms and busts endemic to that industry. It has reinforced this network with extensive corporate support such as emergency parts ordering and shipping that can get a critical item to a stranded farmer within 24 hours, service hotlines, large local parts inventories (those well-financed dealers again), extensive service training programs—the list just goes on. Reflecting this corporate philosophy, Robert Hart, manager of the parts service department at Deere, said, "I've been with Deere for 35 years and, one way or another, they've been very dedicated to providing excellence and service to their customers. They think there's a lot of value in doing that."

## THE CRITICAL DIFFERENCE

Deere's experience demonstrates the vital role that after-sales support plays in keeping the customer happy. In consumer durables such as dishwashers, televisions, automobiles, in industrial machinery, and in office equipment, after-sales support considerations heavily influence brand choice. How well the manufacturer performs in providing this support helps determine customer satisfaction and, ultimately, brand loyalty. Consumers Union assistant director David Berliner thinks, "It goes back to that one word: support. It's to their benefit to make sure that there is a proper and very close to excellent support mechanism out there to which consumers can turn and get satisfaction. It's not good enough for the manufacturer to just sell them the product and then be rid of it."

This is hardly the attitude taken by our winners. For example, Federal Express tries hard to give customers what they want, as explained by Robert Hernandez, vice president of customer service, "If you look at the quality of service, for example, customer inquiries, information. . . . What we do is we tell customers that we're going to respond to their inquiries within 30 minutes or they won't have to pay. Because we know, and it's repeatedly reinforced through letters and customer contacts and surveys, that the information side of this shipment is as important as getting it to that place; I [the customer] have to know what's going on. So the customer base is asking for that, and we say—we have to do it."

Nearly every firm pays at least lip service to the importance of after-sales support. Yet consistently, after-sales support is mentioned as the number one problem area—in automobiles, washing machines, tractors, combines, computers, and telecommunications equipment. Upon analyzing the winners—firms that regularly provide superior after-sales support—we identified three key differences between them and the also rans:

☐ Winners view after-sales support as an opportunity to strengthen their relationship with customers. Most companies view the after-sales support needs of the customer as a necessary evil, something to be disposed of as quickly as possible. By contrast, winners know that "the *real* sale begins after the sale." They realize that customers want and need hand-holding, support, and reassurance after they've purchased a piece of equipment, and these firms are eager to provide it. As Buck Rodgers said in our conversation about IBM, "I think you have to demonstrate value of some kind every day. To me, it can come from the product, from people's courtesy when responding to phone calls, the 24-hour hotlines, the type of maintenance organization you have."

☐ Winners know that the right product design is necessary in meeting after-sales support needs. Otherwise the firm is always playing catch-up—working harder to compensate for basic deficiencies. In the 1970s, Jaguar automobiles were unreliable and difficult to service; both factors raised repair bills and angered customers.

☐ Winners realize that an integrated approach is essential to maximize customer satisfaction with after-sales support and, ultimately, with the overall product. The various elements of product design and after-sales support must complement one another for the best results. Canon's disposable cartridge copiers provide an excellent example: Machine reliability is high enough to make the disposable concept work. The prices of both the copier and the cartridges reduces the customer's financial risk in switching to a new approach. Removing and replacing cartridges is quick, clean, and easy. Finally, the cartridges are readily available. If Canon had failed in creating any one of these support elements—if cartridges were too expensive, difficult to install, or hard to obtain—the entire concept would have collapsed.

## "UNBEATABLE" . . . OR "DEAD ON ARRIVAL"?

After-sales support coupled with a good product yields an unbeatable combination. Poor support plus a mediocre product usually leads to failure—a product that is dead on arrival. Overall, we can identify four common situations (see Figure 8.1).

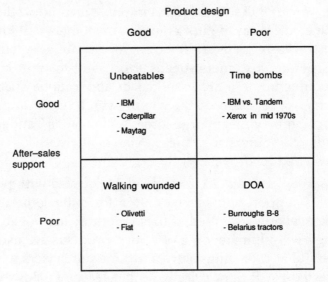

*Figure 8.1 Four common situations*

☐ *Unbeatable.* When good after-sales support is married to a sound product concept, the combination is virtually impossible to beat. Caterpillar, Deere, Maytag, Mercedes-Benz, IBM—all these companies are unbeatable in their respective industries. IBM's 360 series of mainframes, which boosted the company into its preeminent position in the computer industry, provides an excellent illustration. It was good product design—from the *customer's* viewpoint—that allowed for upgrading and expansion and was backed up by superb after-sales support that covered training, applications software, maintenance, updates, and so forth.

☐ *Time Bomb.* A poor product that is propped up by good after-sales support is a time bomb waiting to go off. If the basic design doesn't adequately address key customer needs regarding support, a good after-sales support system merely delays the inevitable. For a limited period customers will be prepared to give the company a second chance.

However, if the firm doesn't improve its product designs, or if a credible competitor emerges, customers will jump ship. In the early 1970s, IBM's designs did not adequately meet corporate customers' needs for a fault-tolerant computer. Such computers are essential in applications such as customer order processing, where even a few minutes' interruption may mean large losses. As soon as Tandem's nonstop computers became a viable alternative, customers switched in droves.

☐ *Walking Wounded.* A good product coupled with poor aftersales support will survive, often for quite some time. But, like walking wounded, if these products are not attended to they will ultimately die off. Such products are usually successful at capturing many first-time purchasers who are attracted by design, price, or other features. However, poor support quality will leave these customers increasingly dissatisfied, and few, if any, will buy the product again. Olivetti's experiences in North America are the classic example. For nearly two decades, Olivetti tried to crack the North American market for office equipment—typewriters, calculators, accounting machines, dedicated word processors. Its products were usually well-designed, innovative, and attractive; several of them won design awards. Its prices provided superior value. However, after-sales support was at best indifferent and often abysmal. Parts weren't available, users were insufficiently trained, manuals were mistranslated or simply inadequate. As a result, Olivetti North America limped along for many years, until it was effectively shut down in 1982.

☐ *Dead on Arrival.* A poor product plus poor after-sales support equals a product that is DOA (dead on arrival). Very little about the product attracts buyers. Those who purchase it do so because they think it's a bargain—and they're immediately disillusioned. Burrough's experience with its B-800 minicomputers (see Chapter 7) is a classic example of a DOA.

## WHY SUPPORT FAILS

Most firms and products are neither unbeatable nor DOA. Instead, they tend to be either walking wounded or time bombs, depending on corporate history. The reasons for this are that many firms:

Are not aware of the importance of after-sales support in customer satisfaction and repeat purchases,

Have not identified or kept up with customers' support needs,

Don't fully understand how customer needs affect both product design and after-sales support, or

Are continuing to use strategies that are no longer appropriate.

## WHAT IS AFTER-SALES SUPPORT?

After-sales support covers all those activities that can help maximize customers' satisfaction after they have purchased the product and started to use it. For consumer durables and for industrial and office equipment, after-sales support includes parts, service, warranty claims, user and service technician training, and, occasionally, even assistance in trading in or otherwise disposing of old equipment. For services, after-sales support may consist of training, emergency assistance (e.g., rapid refunds for stolen travelers' checks), information or status updates (e.g., helping customers locate their packages), and user support (e.g., hotlines for answering questions). For packaged goods, after-sales support covers such things as usage instructions, recipes or suggestions to extend the product beyond its traditional uses, hotlines for emergencies and customer inquiries, and prompt refunds.

Historically, after-sales support activities have been most important and prominent in consumer durables and the industrial and office equipment sectors. In the 1850s custome s were complaining to Cyrus McCormick about the difficulty of obtaining repair parts for their reapers. Similarly, by 1851, the Singer Sewing Machine Company had "begun to set up a vigorous marketing program, which involved using trained women to demonstrate to potential customers the capabilities of the sewing machine. These women also taught buyers or their operators how to use the sewing machine." For many years, Rolls Royce provided classes in driving and maintenance, first for the chauffeurs and later for the owners of its automobiles.

This concentration of after-sales support activities in the equipment and capital goods sectors is easy to understand, once we recognize that the need for after-sales support is related to the stream of benefits we derive (or hope to derive) from a particular product or service. It is when these benefits are interrupted that specific after-sale support needs become tangible. The more valuable this stream of benefits, the greater the importance of after-sales support.

This explains why after-sales support is not particularly significant for the buyer of a candy bar, but it is important to a car buyer and absolutely vital to the purchaser of a tractor. If the candy "fails"—if it is stale or tastes bad—the consumer has lost a small amount of time and money. The car buyer has substantially more at risk, and over a much longer period; he or she may have to live with a lemon for several years, until the next car. For the farmer or industrial contractor purchasing a tractor, the investment made in the equipment pales before the income stream the tractor can help generate; a $60,000 farm tractor is responsible for generating over $1 million in sales over a five-year period.

## WHY IS AFTER-SALES SUPPORT IMPORTANT?

Customers' expectations and concerns regarding after-sales support influence their purchase decisions. Their subsequent experiences have a major impact on their overall satisfaction with the product. In turn, their satisfaction levels determine whether they will buy the same brand again or will switch their loyalties to another manufacturer. After-sales support performance is thus at the heart of customer satisfaction and marketing strategy in consumer durables, in industrial machinery, and in office equipment.

### Farm Equipment

As the survey results discussed at the beginning of this chapter show, after-sales support influences farmers' purchases, affects overall satisfaction, and determines the likelihood that farmers will switch brands.

☐ *After-Sales Support Influences Purchases.* While price was the first consideration in brand choice, mentioned by 43.6 percent of the farmers in the Deere survey, service/dealer was second, mentioned by 26 percent. Product features ranked third, at 15.6 percent, very close to past experience, which was mentioned by 13.7 percent of the respondents. This emphasis on after-sales support in making brand choices has not changed appreciably over the past decades; if anything, farmers are even more inclined to stress after-sales support considerations today than in the past.

☐ *After-Sales Support Determines Satisfaction.* Farmers' overall satisfaction with their purchases is closely related to such after-sales factors as parts availability and resale value. Interestingly, overall satisfaction did not appear to be affected by purchase price or equipment design (features), the two key factors when making the purchase. In addition, as one Deere executive said, "One underlying element of this loyalty [to Deere] is what I would call stability of expectation— and that is one thing that we offer. It's not a real tangible thing that you can nail down, but it just feels like you can always rely on these folks [at Deere]."

☐ *After-Sales Support Determines Brand Loyalty.* Farmers' first preferences, brand loyalty, and willingness to switch were all highly correlated with after-sales support as summarized by the resale price.

The cumulative impact of this pervasive influence of after-sales support on the brands chosen and long-term market share can be great. In 1929, Deere was a distant second to International Harvester in the tractor market, with only 21 percent of the market versus nearly 60 percent for International Harvester. As late as 1959, Deere was still number two with 23 percent of the market. By 1964, Deere was in the lead with a 34 percent share, and it has kept its leadership position ever since.

### Automobiles

For most consumers a car is a significant purchase, perhaps the second largest they will ever make (second only to their house). When something goes wrong it can be very frustrating. As David Berliner of Consumer's Union points out, "It's really a question of where people turn. They're facing a bureaucracy. They see the name of a major auto manufacturer located in Detroit or wherever it may be, and they know there's this chain of command located somewhere in there. They may not know how intricate it is . . . but somewhere down at the bottom is the last person on that chain, that flowchart, and it's the person who sold them that product. . . . They go to that person and they don't get satisfaction and then what do they do? Certainly the person who sold them the product, and wants to get rid of them, is not going to tell them where to go. They won't tell them [the customer] what their next step is, because that'll just come back and haunt them [the dealer]. [For example:] You bring the car in and your expectation is that the person will fix the car, and they make it worse or they don't fix it. Then you're mad at the service station [dealer], but you're also mad, probably, at the manufacturer."

### Home Appliances

Similarly, when purchasing televisions, dishwashers, clothes washers and dryers, or other large home appliances, customers overwhelmingly cite after-sales support as a key consideration in their purchase decisions, their satisfaction levels after the sale and the determination of their next purchase.

## DEFINING AFTER-SALES SUPPORT NEEDS

When customers purchase a product or service, they often believe they are buying more than the specific item; they have expectations regarding the degree of after-sales support the product or service carries with it. This can be as simple as a set of instructions and a throw-away wrench that come with an assemble-it-yourself child's bicycle, or as complicated as warranty programs, service contracts, parts depots, and equipment on loan to replace a defective machine while it is being repaired. Nor are these expectations restricted to consumer durables or industrial and office equipment. Increasingly, customers have expectations regarding the level of after-sales support provided when they purchase micro-computer software, send a package using an overnight delivery service, or open an account at a bank. Buyers of a word-processing or accounting program expect, at the minimum, a user's manual and a tutorial explaining the features of the program; they would also like assistance over the telephone, preferably toll-free. When sending a package overnight, Federal Express's customers have come to expect that they can call and find out when the package will be picked up, its present location, and the likely delivery time. When opening a bank account, we expect to receive accurate monthly statements, assistance in handling emergencies such as stop payments and overdrafts, and other forms of after-sales support.

Companies make several common mistakes when determining

customers' needs for after-sales support. They are unaware of the nonlinearity of expectations regarding support. They tend to concentrate their attention on a single variable such as quality or reliability, ignoring other attributes of support. Finally, they often use averages in measuring support performance, unaware that most support measures tend to be skewed, with a significant proportion of them lying well above the mean.

An additional reason for care in measuring customers' after-sales support expectations lies in the difficulty of interpreting exactly what customers want in terms of variables that are controlled by the manufacturer. For example, the customer's expressed need for more reliability may or may not translate into greater engineering reliabilities. Depending on the circumstances, the customer's desire for greater reliability may actually be related to a number of different sentiments such as "It breaks down too often," "When it breaks down it takes a long time to fix," "It has problems handling all my requirements," or "It didn't last as long as I thought it should have." Except for the first, none of these complaints are directly related to engineering reliability. The consequences of misinterpreting customers' needs can often be quite serious. An industrial equipment manufacturer, for example, invested close to $5 million to improve engineering reliability, only to find out that the major problem was poor parts support.

### Nonlinear Expectations

By and large, we are conditioned to think linearly: If one hour of downtime is bad, two hours are twice as bad. Unfortunately, customer expectations regarding support do not follow this simple logic. Instead, a threshold can be established for many expectations (see Figure 8.2).

During the harvest season, for instance, farmers are extremely sensitive to the length of time a piece of farm equipment is out of commission. Their reactions to downtimes lasting a half-day

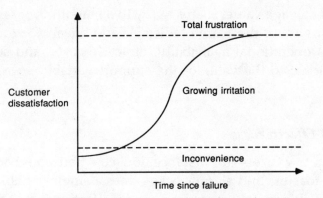

*Figure 8.2 Dissatisfaction with product due to failure*

versus a day or more are vastly different. A failure of a combine that can be repaired in four hours or less is tolerable; in fact, it often provides a welcome respite from harvesting. As the length of downtime increases past four to six hours, however, farmers become concerned, and by eight hours or so, they may be frantic. Beyond eight hours, the actual period of downtime is immaterial; farmers will go to almost any lengths to get up and running again—even if it means purchasing another combine.

Farmers appear to have a similar threshold regarding the frequency with which a combine fails. Naturally, they hope it never fails; but being realists, they're willing to accept an average of one or two failures per season. Farmers' tolerance of failure decreases very rapidly beyond this point, however, so that a combine design averaging three or four failures per season acquires a poor reputation. This attitude appears to be independent of the downtime duration at each failure; the number of failures is what the farmers remember, not how quickly the repairs were made.

Not all support expectations have clear thresholds. For instance, customers expect gradual improvements in the operational availability of a product or service (i.e., in its effective use during a given period). Since expected life-cycle costs—the purchase costs combined with discounted maintenance and repair costs less discounted salvage value, if any—vary in a smooth progression, expectations about these are predictable and linear. Customer reactions (to operational availability, life-cycle costs, and so on) are proportional to the value of the support variable.

### Support Effectiveness

In only a few cases—for instance, low-cost household appliances such as toasters and alarm clocks—does a single variable such as reliability adequately measure support effectiveness. The farmer measures the support provided to his or her combine or tractor in terms of at least two variables—failure frequency and downtime per failure. The sophisticated purchaser of electronic office equipment weighs the support packages available as well as the training and programming assistance provided.

Moreover, customer preferences are often noncompensatory. Customers rank-order their preferences and do not consider an excess of one type of support as a substitute for deficiencies in another. A contractor buying a bulldozer, for example, wants both high reliability and low downtime per failure. He or she will be dissatisfied with any equipment that causes excessive downtime per failure, no matter how infrequently the failure occurs. Similarly, the office equipment buyer wants rapid response, irrespective of how infrequently it may be needed. For both, the risks and requirements of downtime are too high.

### Statistical Averages

One customer may get a car that's problem-free, another a lemon or a succession of lemons. Parts can be obtained over the counter—right away or 10 days later. To cope with the random fluctuations, people tend to use the average or the mean: the mean wage rate, the mean time between failures, and so forth.

In our investigations, we found ample evidence that averages are not only misleading but potentially dangerous when used to measure support effectiveness. An industrial equipment company, for example, prided itself on the apparently high reliability of its product. Engineering tests indicated that the mean time between failures for its major product was 400 hours. Since the average annual use was 600 hours, management felt satisfied; after all, the machine experienced only between one and two failures per year.

On conducting a survey of users, however, the company received a rude shock. True enough, the average number of failures was 1.65 per year. But more than 40 percent of the users reported more than two failures a year; and of those, 20 percent had four or more failures. As the sales vice president put it, "If it's true, over 40 percent of our customers are not happy with our performance!"

This situation is also true of other support measures such as downtime per failure. These measures tend to be distributed in a skewed fashion, with a significant proportion of them lying well above the mean. For this reason, the mean is an extremely misleading measure. A more appropriate measure is percentile, such as the 80th or 90th percentile of the variable in question. This measure would have shown the industrial equipment company that a large proportion of its users were in fact experiencing more than two failures per year. Similarly, the office equipment company that assured purchasers, "We can usually have a service person out to your location within four to six hours," would have found that response time in the 80th percentile was closer to two working days.

## THE KEY DRIVERS

We can better understand customers' needs if we analyze the underlying costs, using the life-cycle cost concept employed in equipment purchasing decisions. As discussed earlier, after-sales support becomes important when the product offers a continuing stream of benefits for a significant period after the purchase. The life of the product can then be viewed as a sequence of uptimes and downtimes, terminated eventually by a final failure, obsolescence, or sale. As the product goes through this cycle, customers incur repair costs due to failure, maintenance costs, opportunity costs related to the loss of benefits during downtime, and costs related to uncertainty about the length and frequency of failures, the time needed for repair and the magnitude of costs incurred.

We can broadly group these costs into two categories: costs that are independent of the duration of the failure (or **fixed costs**), and those that vary with the length of the failure (or **variable costs**).

**Fixed costs** of failure are (1) *repair costs* related to the actual repair of the equipment or system, that is, parts and labor, (2) *transactions costs* related to placing orders for parts, repair services, and so on; and (3) *information costs* related to uncertainties. Repair costs are usually out-of-pocket costs, especially for consumer durables, unless the product is under warranty. The other two categories of costs are not easily identifiable and, in some cases, can only be measured implicitly through premiums paid for a particular supplier or specific service support methodology. For example, it can be argued that the purchaser of a service contract seeks to reduce transaction and information costs. The premium the buyer pays for the contract over the expected repair expense is an aggregate measure of these costs.

**Variable costs** of failure can be subdivided into (1) *out-of-pocket costs* and (2) opportunity costs. Out-of-pocket costs are nonrepair-related expenditures directly incurred as a result of equipment failure that vary with the duration of the failure. Examples are wages that have to be paid to workers waiting on a stalled earthmover or to programmers who are idled by a computer "crash." These costs can be quite high. In one survey, farmers estimated their out-of-pocket costs at between $50 and $100 per hour. For an industrial contractor they could be even higher, between $500 and $1000 an hour, and for an airline, they may amount to several thousands of dollars per hour.

Opportunity costs are those costs incurred by the diversion of resources from other, more productive uses and the reduction in output caused by failure. Examples are the revenues forgone by an airline in keeping aircraft idle as stand-bys and the lower levels of output obtained by farmers with equipment problems during planting and harvesting.

By analyzing the fixed and variable costs incurred by purchasers of a particular product, we can understand why and to what degree customers' expectations are nonlinear, how purchasers rank-order their preferences, and why averages are misleading. If a customer's variable costs of failure are significant, then beyond a certain time interval he or she must act to limit the likely damage from continued service interruption, or else the losses will be overwhelming. Consequently, once that stage is reached, the customer stops worrying about the product that has failed and starts lining up alternatives—purchasing a used combine, for example, or renting a word processor. The time it takes the customer to reach this stage depends on the magnitude of these costs: The higher the costs, the shorter the interval. Similarly, the relative importance of the fixed and variable costs on failure determines how customers rank-order preferences. A householder is extremely concerned about fixed costs and has relatively low variable costs upon failure; consequently he or she will require high reliability rates and low repair bills. A builder, on the other hand, is much more concerned about downtime, and wants a balance between high reliability and low downtime per failure.

Fixed and variable costs of failure also help define four segments—corresponding to the combinations of high fixed/low variable, low fixed/high variable, and so on—in which the optimal product and after-sales support strategies are radically different. However, in order to determine these optimal strategies, we must first understand the generic after-sales support strategies that companies employ.

## GENERIC SUPPORT STRATEGIES

Firms use a variety of approaches in meeting customers' after-sales support needs. Broadly speaking, these can be classified into three groups: Those that are product- or design-related, those that concentrate on the support system, and those that concentrate on reducing uncertainty.

**Product- or design-related** strategies are of three generic types: those focusing on product *reliability*, those changing the product design to make it more *modular* in construction, and those that build in *redundancy*.

- ☐ *Reliability improvement* lowers the customer's total costs. This is usually the first approach used by firms in improving service support.

- ☐ *Modular design* can lower variable costs by making the equipment easier to repair. The entire product is divided into a series of modules or components, many or all of which can be removed and repaired or replaced. This approach was first popularized in electronics and now has spread to other industries. It often is termed swap-out maintenance.

- ☐ *Built-in redundancy* means that the product or system is designated to have two or more of each critical system or component; in case one fails, the back-up takes over and maintains service. Originally used in aircraft, this strategy is catching on in computers, as with Tandem's nonstop computing, and other equipment. Cars, for example, now have dual braking systems so that if one fails, the other can take over and prevent catastrophe.

**Support system-related** strategies concentrate on changing the way in which service is provided. These strategies can be grouped into the following two subcategories:

- ☐ Improvements in system response times help to clear what often is a major bottleneck. Companies can improve the speed with which the support system reacts to a failure by adding service technicians, moving them closer to customers (in some case, onto customers' premises), and providing rapid handling of emergency parts orders.

☐ Reductions in equipment repair times complement reductions in response time. Companies can reduce actual repair times by providing improved service technician training, on-site (or even built-in) diagnostic equipment, fully equipped mobile repair vans, a design change to a modular repair philosophy, or loaners.

**Strategies that reduce customer's risks** can improve after-sales support and customer satisfaction by controlling or eliminating the potential for significant financial losses due to product malfunction. They can be further subdivided into *warranties* and *service contracts*.

☐ *Warranties* are used to (1) reduce customers' out-of-pocket costs during the immediate postpurchase period and (2) allay any fears customers may have regarding product reliability. Both the terms of the warranties and their duration vary considerably from industry to industry and, within a given industry, from company to company. On occasion warranties may be used as defensive weapons to allay customers' fears about the viability of a firm, as was the case with Chrysler's five-year/50,000-mile warranty and Jaguar's 24-month, unlimited warranty.

☐ *Service contracts* are used to reduce buyers' uncertainties about maintenance costs. These contracts are more prevalent in the office equipment, telecommunications, and computer industries than in other industries. In the beginning, service contracts were fairly uniform and the customer had few alternatives; today, for most types of equipment, there are a number of service contract options, including purchase of contracts from third parties independent of the equipment manufacturers.

## THE NEED FOR AN INTEGRATED APPROACH

Many companies use these generic strategies haphazardly, either singly or in combination, without fully understanding their interactions and implications. Management will typically aim simultaneously to improve reliability, increase parts availability, reduce repair times, and, for good measure, cut product costs. Consequently, while a great deal of money may be spent, there is little tangible improvement in after-sales support or customer satisfaction. The reasons behind this lack of integration include the following:

☐ *An Explicit Strategy Is Lacking.* After-sales support is viewed as a collection of individual tasks—reliability improvement, technician training, and so on. Improving support therefore means more of the same.

☐ *Responsibility for Support Is Diffused.* As a result, management receives a disjointed picture of after-sales support and its relation both to customer needs and to the company's product strategy.

☐ *Support Needs Are Considered Late in the Development Cycle.* This leads to many last-minute modifications to design and lowers customer satisfaction. In the mid-1970s, changing spark plugs on a certain Detroit product meant that the entire engine had to be jacked up.

☐ *Management Focuses on Individual Support Attributes.* Diffusion of responsibility causes management to focus on internal matters—parts availability, warranty costs, service training—rather than on customer satisfaction per se.

The U.S. Navy's experiences with the JT7D turbine used in its PF class of frigates provides an excellent example of what happens when various elements of after-sales support are not matched with each other. In the 1970s, the Navy used this gas turbine as an auxiliary power unit on its new class of frigates. This was a change from the previous practice of using diesel engines to provide auxiliary power. The rationale for the change was that fewer moving parts in the new turbine would provide greater reliability. Unfortunately, what no one realized at the time was that the turbine manufacturer had designed the equipment with a "remove, repair, and replace" strategy in mind. In other words, in order to carry out major repairs on the turbine it was necessary first to remove the entire turbine. But to its horror, the Navy found out that it did not have enough access space to remove the turbine; it had assumed that the turbine would be repaired in place, in accordance with standard Navy practice. The solution: Cut a hole in the side of the ship.

Jaguar's experiences in the 1970s also illustrate the need for an integrated approach. Although its automobile's basic design was attractive, overall customer satisfaction was continuously slipping, to the point that by 1980, Jaguar wasn't even rated on a customer satisfaction index survey conducted by a major automotive marketing research firm. To quote Neal Johnson, sales and marketing director of Jaguar, "Sales were going down. . . . It was clear to everybody that something had to be done. The weakest part of the Jaguar problem was not the style of the car or the color of the car or any of those things, but the quality. It wasn't engineering's problem or service's problem or manufacturing's problem, it was *everybody's* [emphasis added] problem." Getting customer satisfaction to make a U-turn, as Jaguar did in the period from 1980 to 1984, therefore required attention to every element of after-sales support. Product reliability had to be improved. Along with that, it was essential to upgrade parts availability, service facilities at the dealer level, overall warranty program, and warranty administration.

## DESIGNING UNBEATABLE STRATEGIES

We can use the fixed and variable costs incurred by the customer when a product fails to develop a conceptual framework that

Integrates the various elements of product design and after-sales support,

Identifies four support-related segments (disposables, repairables, never fails, and fast response), and

Defines optimal design and after-sales support strategies for each segment.

To see how this works, we can plot various products on a grid in terms of their relative fixed and variable costs. For instance:

☐ Small household appliances such as toasters and radios have low or no repair costs; typically, it is cheaper to replace them when they fail. Their variable costs of failure are also very low, because owners have costless alternatives. Thus such appliances fall in the low/low quadrant. (See Figure 8.3.)

☐ Large appliances such as washers, dryers, automobiles, and large television sets can have significant repair costs associated with them; rarely will the purchaser prefer to scrap the item rather than repair it. However, they have relatively low variable costs of failure, either because the owner does not incur real out-of-pocket costs, or because the owner has low-cost alternatives (e.g., the nearby laundromat, or a cheap car rental). Consequently, such items fall in the low/high quadrant.

☐ Most industrial and office equipment such as tractors, combines, and copiers cause significant repair and downtime costs when they fail. However, typically the cost per hour of downtime (e.g., the wages of crews idled by the shutdown, lost crops, copying or printing purchased from the outside,

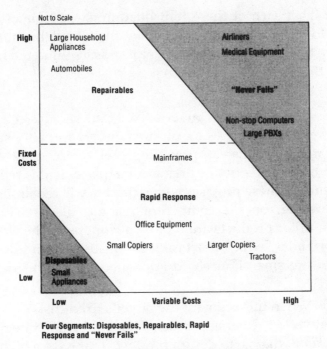

Four Segments: Disposables, Repairables, Rapid
Response and "Never Fails"

*Figure 8.3 Implications for product design*

and so forth) is substantially higher than the repair costs.
Therefore such items fall in the high/low quadrant.

☐ Airplanes, large mainframes and PBXs, hospital intensive
care equipment have very high repair and service interruption costs. In some cases failure can be literally catastrophic.
These products therefore fall into the high/high quadrant.

### Disposables and Never Fails

If we now analyze the characteristics of winners in each of these
four groupings, we find that (1) the key factors for success differ,
(2) there is usually an unbeatable product and after-sales support
strategy for each quadrant, and (3) companies that follow other
strategies either have time bombs or walking wounded on their
hands.

We can label each of these four quadrants, or regimes. We will call the low/low regime the *disposables,* the low/high regime the *repairables,* the high/low regime the *rapid response,* and the high/high regime the *never-fails.*

1. *Disposables.* When the buyer's fixed and variable costs of failure are very low, a *disposable* product design and after-sales support strategy dominates—providing that replacement costs are low and the buyer's risk of premature replacement is reduced. In the absence of these provisions, purchasers will repair their products; however, once a competitor using a disposable strategy emerges, other products are rapidly abandoned. The classic case is that of Timex, which practically eliminated watch repair; other examples are small household appliances and industrial instruments.

2. *Repairable.* In this segment the buyer's fixed costs of failure are high relative to the variable costs. The dominant strategy then is *high reliability,* that is, to design products that have a high level of reliability (although not as high as disposables) and keep out-of-pocket repair costs low. Examples of companies following this strategy include: Maytag in premium appliances, Whirlpool in mass-market appliances, most Japanese automakers in compact automobiles, and Mercedes-Benz in luxury cars. Ease of repair is relatively secondary to inherent/design reliability and manufacturing costs.

3. *Rapid Response.* When variable costs of failure are of prime importance, the dominant strategy is one that uses product design and support systems to reduce total downtime. In general, this requires a balanced approach, such as modularity in product design and rapid logistic system response. Superiority along only one dimension, such as reliability, tends to be suboptimal. Caterpillar, Deere, and IBM are leaders in implementing such balanced strategies.

4. *Never Fails.* When both the fixed and variable costs of failure are high, a *never-fail* design and/or support strategy is dominant.

Typically this requires system- or component-level redundancy to virtually eliminate any benefit interruptions; if one component or system fails, a backup takes over while the failure is repaired. Where this is not technologically or economically feasible, strategies such as stringent (hard-time) periodic maintenance, continuous monitoring, and on-site repair personnel are used. However, whenever a competitor uses redundancy it becomes the dominant strategy. For example, in certain computing applications where nonstop performance is essential, Tandem's redundant designs have displaced IBM's more conventional approaches.

The advantage of this framework is that it covers all products and services for which after-sales support is an important consideration. Therefore any conclusions we draw from it have broad applications.

1. *One Strategy Dominates All Others in Each Regime*, with One Possible Exception: Rapid Response. For the disposable, high-reliability, and never-fail regimes, we can determine in advance the best product and after-sales support strategies. In the disposable segment, the best strategy is very high reliability combined with low manufacturing costs; the repairability is not very important. After-sales support should be handled through an extended warranty. The key to success is the ability to build products that have high reliability at low production cost. At the other extreme, in the never-fail regime, the key is to design against any and all potential failures, within the constraints of affordability. The after-sales support strategy has to be modified appropriately depending on the specific design. For example, most commercial aircraft have multiple systems—avionic, hydraulic, and electrical. There is built-in redundancy in the design. This is supported with maintenance at defined, scheduled intervals. Fault-tolerant computers take a different approach; here, a combination of hardware and software redundancy is built in to eliminate the possibility of failure. For repairables the best strategy combines high reliability with relatively easy access for repairs. The only exception is the

rapid-response regime, comprising such goods as tractors, large copiers, various types of office equipment, mainframe computers, and so forth. In this case, it is difficult to state *a priori* which approach is best. Depending on the relative importance of the various costs of failure, strategies such as loaners, modular exchange of components, high reliability, or a combination of all of these are best.

2. *The Keys to Success Are Substantially Different in Each Regime.* In the disposable regime, it is essential to keep the total price of the product below the threshold at which customers will pay for repair, while maintaining high enough reliability so that dissatisfaction is kept to a minimum. On the other hand, in the rapid-response regime, success hinges on the ability to improve the total system performance, that is, matching product design, manufacturing, and after-sales support to deliver the least amount of downtime in the field at an acceptable cost. Table 8.1 summarizes differences in customer concerns, product strategy, after-sales support strategy, and the keys to success in each of these four areas.

3. *Shifts from One Regime to Another Are of Crucial Importance.* Tandem shifted one segment of mainframe computers from rapid response to never fail and created a new niche not dominated by IBM. Canon made tremendous inroads into Xerox's hold on the small copier market by introducing the disposable cartridge for copiers. Overnight, Xerox's main strength—its extensive sales and support network—became a liability. Now nearly any dealer could sell Canon copiers without having to invest substantial sums of money in technician training, parts inventories, and so on. Customers overall were happier: Secretaries no longer got their hands dirty handling toner, copies didn't smudge, there was no mess. Similarly, the dramatic reductions in the price of personal computers have moved word-processing machines from the rapid-response regime to a combination of never fails and repairables. Only five years ago, a dedicated word processor carried a price tag of $10,000 or more and cost at least $1000 per year in

| Segment | Key Customer Concerns | Product Strategy | Support Strategy | Keys for Success | Examples |
|---|---|---|---|---|---|
| "Disposables" | High Reliability<br>Low Replacement Costs | Very High Reliability<br>Low Manufacturing Costs<br>Repairability Not Important | 1–2 Year Warranty | Very High Reliability<br>Low Product Cost<br>Credibility, Reliability, Warranty | Timex |
| "Repairables" | High Reliability<br>Moderate/Low Expected Repair Costs<br>Low Skill Requirements/ Easily Available Service | High Design Reliability<br>Repairability Important in Design | Conventional: i.e., On-site<br>Wide Availability e.g., Do-it-yourself Kits, Third-party Service, etc. | High Reliability<br>Design Simplicity<br>Low Repair Costs | Maytag<br>Sears/Whirlpool |
| "Rapid Response" | Downtime/ Failure<br>Operational Availability<br>Service Support Costs | Balance:<br>—reliability<br>—ease of repair<br>Standardize Parts to Lower Logistics Costs | Mix:<br>—loaners<br>—on-site maintenance<br>Maintain High Fill Rates in Logistic System | Ability to Choose Most Cost-effective Mixture of Design and Support | Caterpillar<br>Deere |
| "Never Fail" | Protection Against Any and All Failures/ Interruptions<br>Affordability | "Fault-tolerant" Design<br>Built-in or Add-on Redundance<br>Delivery to Acceptable Cost | Back-up Maintenance<br>Inspection/ Replacement | Very High Component Reliability<br>Cost-effective Design<br>Credibility | Tandem |

maintenance. Today, most firms can purchase a personal computer for almost the cost of the annual service contract. Today it is more economical for a firm to replace the dedicated word processor and on-site maintenance contract with two personal computers and a carry-in service contract. If one of the computers fails and has to be repaired, the firm can continue operations with the other.

As these and other examples indicate, whenever a manufacturer changes its design and after-sales support strategy from one regime to the other, there could be major structural changes in the industry. If the shift is successful, customers' expectations regarding after-sales support will change dramatically and customers of companies who stick with the older designs are likely to experience high levels of dissatisfaction. The product design determines the maximum level of after-sales satisfaction the customer will receive. Firms that choose a wrong or outdated approach start with a severe handicap; most of their after-sales activities will be aimed at overcoming the deficiencies of the basic design and reducing customer discontent.

Timex is the ultimate example of a completely integrated business, product, and after-sales support strategy. In 1949, when United States Time (as Timex was then called) introduced its first Timex watches, the Swiss watchmaking industry dominated the world market. The Swiss watch was a classic example of the repairable strategy: The watches were relatively expensive, were sold almost exclusively through jewelers, and required periodic cleaning and, occasionally, repairs. Timex's strategy was the very opposite: The company made a disposable watch that was still reliable enough to be acceptable. The company was selling "not elegance or prestige but cheap time, and at those prices people could afford not one watch but two or three or more." Everything that Timex did supported this disposable strategy:

- ☐ Timex simplified its designs to the extreme; as one of the managers put it, "When you put a watch together with relatively unskilled labor, it must be able to run accurately the minute the last wheel is put in place. We can't afford the petty, troublesome adjustments that are found in the handmade watch industry."

- ☐ Timex's pricing was value for money. The first, simple models sold at $6.95 to $7.95—about one-tenth of the price of a good Swiss watch.

- ☐ Timex sold these watches in every available retail outlet: pharmacies, supermarkets, variety stores, airport shops, hardware stores, tobacconists—a quarter of a million points of sale at the peak.

- ☐ The after-sales support strategy was simple: a long warranty (typically a year). At the end of that period, if the watch stopped running, the owner simply threw it away. Timex cases were riveted and couldn't be opened for repair.

In short, everything—design, manufacturing, pricing, channels of distribution, warranties—aligned with this disposable approach. Its success was overwhelming: in 1962, 13 years after the first Timex was introduced, the company's U.S. market share exceeded 30 percent. By 1973, Timex had 45 percent of the U.S. market. The Swiss manufacturers who until then had dominated the world market for watches had to abandon the mass market and restrict their activities to a few high-priced lines, essentially becoming jewelers.

# 9

# *Feedback and Restitution*

Many companies don't realize that customer complaints can be more than a grave problem. They are also a tremendous opportunity. If customers who complain are ignored or treated unsatisfactorily, they can become a threat to the company's franchise. On the other hand, if their needs are addressed effectively, these same customers represent significant future sales.

Customer dissatisfaction presents a serious threat because many unhappy customers don't complain—at least, not to the company. Instead they tell family and friends about their dissatisfaction. A good number of them switch to other suppliers. If and when they do complain to the company, they are pessimistic about their chances of being satisfied. The company's response frequently confirms their worst suspicions.

The result is that the company and its customers become increasingly isolated from each other. Management thinks that because there are no complaints, there are no problems. Lacking information from the customer about the causes of dissatisfaction—poor product design, low manufacturing quality, bad sales practices, misleading advertising, inadequate after-sales support—the company repeats its mistakes. Customers, in turn, grow more frustrated with what they see as the company's indifference to their problems and needs, and switch to other suppliers.

Handled effectively, however, complaints provide the company with opportunities to retain customers who otherwise might switch, to increase customer satisfaction and positive word-of-mouth advertising, and to obtain valuable information about the underlying causes of dissatisfaction.

The impact of proper complaint treatment on sales can be dramatic. A study conducted in 1981 for Coca-Cola found that "1.56 customers were gained as a result of positive word-of-mouth communication for every customer lost . . . following Coca-Cola's responses."

Equally important, complaints provide information about perceived and actual problems and strengthen the links between the firm and its customers. By analyzing the complaints, managers can deal with the causes of the problems by making design changes, improving quality, instituting better communications, and so forth. These actions show customers that the firm is responsive to their needs and concerns, which increases customers' satisfaction with the company's products and services. Instead of drifting apart, the company and its customers come closer together.

To cope with this apparent paradox—customer complaints as both threat and opportunity—businesses must recognize the following:

- ☐ Customers don't complain.
- ☐ Customers are pessimistic about how companies will deal with their problems.
- ☐ Corporate behavior tends to confirm their pessimism.

☐ Customers want to be treated fairly.

☐ How companies respond to complaints greatly affects customer satisfaction and loyalty.

☐ Companies must shift from handling complaints to communicating with customers to maximize customer satisfaction.

## CUSTOMERS DON'T COMPLAIN

Those customers who do complain generally represent a minority among the number of dissatisfied buyers. Table 9.1 details the results of a major survey, showing, for various products, the percentages of customers who were dissatisfied but didn't complain. We find that anywhere from 71 percent (in the cases of auto repair

**TABLE 9.1  Selected Product/Service Category and Course of Action**

| Type of Product | Third Party Complainer | Second Party Complainer | No Action |
|---|---|---|---|
| | (N = 113) | (N = 1297) | (N = 1422) |
| Auto | 2% | 21% | 77% |
| Mail-order service | 1 | 22 | 77 |
| Radio and television | 1 | 17 | 82 |
| Food and groceries | 1 | 15 | 84 |
| Furniture | 1 | 16 | 83 |
| Household | a | a | a |
| Clothing | b | 13 | 87 |
| House repairs | 4 | 21 | 74 |
| Appliances | 0 | 12 | 88 |
| Auto repairs | 1 | 28 | 71 |

a Comparable product/service categories could not be constructed.

b These percentages are less than .5%.

Source: Best, A., and Andreasen, A.R. *Talking Back to Business: Voiced and Unvoiced Consumer Complaints* (Washington, DC: Center for Study of Responsive Law, 1976). Read as "percentage of all problems reported with the product."

customers) to about 90 percent (among buyers of clothing and appliances) of customers with problems didn't complain. The Center for the Study of Responsive Law (CSRL), an organization affiliated with various consumerist groups, has found that "buyers suppress complaints regarding two-thirds of the problems they perceive."

### Why Don't Customers Complain?

Overwhelmingly, customers don't complain because they don't believe it will do any good. Consistently, their reasons are, "It's too much hassle," "It doesn't do any good," or "It isn't worth all the time and trouble." One writer explained, "Complaints require the expenditure of time, money, and effort, resources which are in short supply for most people . . . complaint behavior was highly rational, usually involving high-cost goods and services."

Two factors in particular make it difficult for customers to complain: *lack of knowledge* and *frustration with complaint mechanisms*. For example: Consumers Union receives about 50,000 calls and letters a year from customers with problems. The vast majority of people turn to Consumers Union because they don't know where else to go. According to David Berliner of Consumers Union, "The number one problem is that people just don't know how to complain and when to complain. They have something wrong . . . they're frustrated, they're angry, they want satisfaction . . . they want to get the thing resolved and they don't know where to turn."

He continued with, "Once you get past the barrier and people know where to turn, then it's a question of 'How do you pursue it?' It's not readily available data—at least, it's not on the side of the product saying, 'If you're not happy, go to your dealer, and if your dealer doesn't give you satisfaction, call the zone representative,' and on down the line. They don't tell you that."

## Who Complains and When?

Generally, customers are less likely to complain about low-cost, frequently purchased items than about more expensive, infrequently purchased goods. The less important the product, the less likely the customer is to complain. Researchers also have found that customers with certain demographic characteristics are more likely to complain than are other people. Specifically:

☐ Poor or less educated customers are less likely to complain, in part because they tend to be less aware of how and to whom to complain.

☐ Higher-income and more educated customers are more likely to complain; this propensity is also linked to level of political activity and awareness.

☐ The more expensive the product or the problem, the more likely people will complain, which suggests that customers know that complaining can be difficult and costly.

## What Do Customers Complain About?

A CSRL study found that customers complain about, in descending order of frequency, defective products or services, false or misleading advertising, purchases not measuring up to expected standards, and misrepresentation of financial arrangements (i.e., credit and billing). Consumers Union has found five major subjects of complaints. In descending order of frequency, they are refusal of credit, billing for deceptive goods, automobiles (including warranty and service problems), appliances, and packaged goods.

## To Whom Do Customers Complain?

The vast majority of customers who complain do so to someone at the point of sale. Furthermore, they are more favorably disposed toward the manufacturer than are customers who initially get in touch with third parties such as government agencies, the Better Business Bureau, the Consumer Product Safety Commission, or a lawyer (see Table 9.2). In other words, customers who make contact with a third party immediately are likely to be more angry and require more compensation to be satisfied than customers who first bring their complaints to the point of sale.

When dissatisfied customers don't complain to the seller, manufacturer, or third parties, what do they do?

First, they tend to change their brands or the places at which they shop, or both. Second, they tell others—their neighbors, relatives, friends.

### Customers Switch

Many customers who are unhappy don't fight; they just switch. When A.C. Nielsen surveyed purchasers of various packaged goods, it found that:

☐ One in four dissatisfied customers refused to buy the brand again, and

**TABLE 9.2 *Attribution of Responsibility Magnitude of Problem***

|  |  | Third Party | Second Party Complainers | No Action Complainers |
|---|---|---|---|---|
| Felt place of service was responsible: | No | 51 | 65 | 72 |
|  | Yes | 49 | 35 | 28 |
| Felt place of purchase was responsible: | No | 75 | 57 | 55 |
|  | Yes | 25 | 43 | 45 |
| Felt manufacturer was responsible: | No | 96 | 79 | 79 |
|  | Yes | 4 | 21 | 21 |

*Source*: Grainer, Marc A. *et al.* "Consumer Problems and Complaints: A National View," in *Advances in Consumer Research, Vol. 6*, William L. Wilkie, ed., 1978, pp. 494–500.

☐ One in five refused to buy that particular product or that type of product again.

Obviously, a number of factors determine whether dissatisfied customers will change brands: the availability of alternatives, the seriousness of the problem, what attempts (if any) the firm has made to solve the problem, and so forth. But the basic impulse is still the same: to switch rather than fight. For example: Nearly half of the dissatisfied customers in a 1979 survey of automobile owners indicated that they would not purchase another car from the same manufacturer. This even affects customers that are brand loyal; 25 percent of those who said they would not purchase another car from the same manufacturer had bought their last two cars from that company.

### Customers Tell Others

Most of us have seen the sign, "If you're happy with our service, tell others; if not, tell us." Dissatisfied customers appear to stand this saying on its head. When they're upset they tell their friends, neighbors, relatives—everybody but the manufacturer.

☐ When undergraduates at a university in the western United States were surveyed about their clothing purchases, researchers found that a student who was dissatisfied spoke to, on average, five individuals about the problem. Eighty-five percent mentioned their problems to at least one other individual. In nearly all cases, they described the problem. Two-thirds of the time they remembered the name of the store where the problem occurred and in about half of the cases they mentioned the brand of the clothing. Ironically, they mentioned the store's response only a third of the time.

☐ Hotel guests surveyed in a city in the northeastern United

States indicated that two out of three times they'd mention the complaint to their friends or associates. Nearly half (47 percent) said they would be highly likely to caution others not to use the hotel.

## CUSTOMERS' EXPECTATIONS ARE LOW

When consumers do complain, they do not have much hope of receiving satisfaction. For example, a survey of customers who complained to a clothing manufacturer showed that:

Eleven percent of the customers didn't know how the retailer from whom they purchased the item would react;

More then one-third of the complainers bypassed the retailer and went directly to the manufacturer; and

Thirty-three percent of those who got in touch with the manufacturer didn't know how the firm would react.

The results of another survey were equally revealing. Students at three universities in Michigan, Oregon, and southern California wrote to manufacturers about an actual problem they had with a recent product or service purchase. The responses, if any, from these manufacturers and service providers were then analyzed. Several interesting facts emerged.

☐ The participants expected that fewer than half of the companies would respond to their complaint letters. They were close: only 56 percent replied.

☐ One-third of the students expected that they would receive an apology, while 17 percent thought they would get only a token response.

☐ Overall, both those who received a response and those who didn't were not disappointed. Nearly one-half (46.4 percent) of those who received a response said it was "about as expected," while more than 63 percent of those who didn't receive a response had not expected one anyhow.

These attitudes are representative of consumers generally. In the period 1971 to 1979, two researchers conducted four surveys, spaced two years apart, of consumers' attitudes toward business. Respondents were asked whether they agreed or disagreed with various statements regarding product quality, advertising, selling

**TABLE 9.3   Attitudes Toward Consumerism, 1971 to 1979**

|  | Year of Survey | Percentage of Consumers | | | | |
|---|---|---|---|---|---|---|
|  |  | Strongly Agree | Agree | Uncertain | Disagree | Strongly Disagree |
| *When consumers have* | 1971 | 2 | 14 | 15 | 52 | 17 |
| *problems with* | 1973 | 1 | 17 | 16 | 53 | 13 |
| *products they have* | 1975 | 1 | 21 | 18 | 48 | 12 |
| *purchased, it is* | 1977 | 1 | 22 | 21 | 46 | 10 |
| *usually easy to get* | 1979 | 0 | 22 | 18 | 50 | 10 |
| *them corrected.* |  |  |  |  |  |  |
| *Most business firms* | 1971 | 4 | 53 | 21 | 18 | 4 |
| *make a sincere* | 1973 | 2 | 55 | 21 | 20 | 2 |
| *effort to adjust* | 1975 | 3 | 56 | 23 | 15 | 3 |
| *consumer* | 1977 | 3 | 58 | 23 | 14 | 2 |
| *complaints fairly.* | 1979 | 3 | 55 | 21 | 19 | 2 |
| *From the consumer's* | 1971 | 13 | 54 | 16 | 16 | 1 |
| *viewpoint, the* | 1973 | 13 | 51 | 18 | 17 | 1 |
| *procedures followed* | 1975 | 12 | 49 | 17 | 21 | 1 |
| *by most* | 1977 | 11 | 47 | 20 | 22 | 0 |
| *manufacturers in* | 1979 | 10 | 48 | 23 | 18 | 1 |
| *handling complaints* |  |  |  |  |  |  |
| *and settling* |  |  |  |  |  |  |
| *grievances of* |  |  |  |  |  |  |
| *consumers are not* |  |  |  |  |  |  |
| *satisfactory.* |  |  |  |  |  |  |

*Source*: Barksdale, H.C., and W.D. Perrault, Jr. in *MSU Business Topics*, Spring 1980, p. 27.

practices, and so on. Consistently, customers showed a very skeptical, if not pessimistic, attitude about business' response to complaints (see Table 9.3).

☐ Nearly two-thirds of the respondents didn't think that product problems could be corrected easily.

☐ Forty percent were uncertain about or disagreed with the proposition that "most firms make a sincere effort to adjust consumer complaints fairly."

☐ Two-thirds were not satisfied with companies' procedures for handling complaints and settling grievances.

Most disturbing was the fact that three out of four respondents agreed with the statement, "The exploitation of consumers by business firms deserves more attention than it receives."

## CUSTOMERS' PESSIMISM IS JUSTIFIED

Consumers have reason to be skeptical of companies. For example, in the previous experiment, in which manufacturers' responses to students' complaints were analyzed, 14 percent of the companies sent out a form letter, 3.6 percent sent literature, and 36 percent sent a personal letter. Only in 7 percent of the cases were the customers' questions answered.

Corporate executives appear to be complacent about their handling of customer complaints. A 1976 survey of 400 executives nationwide and 1200 New York state consumers indicated:

Eighty-five percent of the executives (vs. only 51 percent of the consumers) believed that "most firms make good on warranty claims," and

Eighty-four percent of the executives (vs. only 54 percent of the consumers) believed that "most firms make a sincere effort to adjust . . . complaints fairly."

In the same survey, 85 percent of the executives agreed with the statement that "many of the mistakes consumers make in buying products are the results of their own carelessness."

### Companies Are Often Defensive

Frequently firms are defensive and even hostile about customer feedback and restitution. The U.S. Post Office, for example, wants to see the original receipt for late Express Mail deliveries before it will refund the money. Further, it will make the refund only at the originating post office. Contrast this with Federal Express, which credits the sender's account almost immediately for a late delivery.

Typical symptoms of this negative corporate attitude include:

- ☐ Cumbersome or complex complaint procedures
- ☐ A slow and grudging approach to refunds and repairs
- ☐ Numerous exceptions in warranty policies
- ☐ An adversarial approach to dealing with customer complaints
- ☐ Delays in making necessary changes in products or services

Ford was extremely slow in changing the design of the gas tank in its Pinto, despite several lawsuits and many internal indications that the design was dangerous. Even the best firms are not immune: IBM stuck with its unpopular, "chiclet"-style keyboard for the PCjr personal computer for far too long.

## The Complaints Department Has Low Status

In many companies the customer complaints department is an internal Siberia, a dead end. It is often in a staff function (e.g., legal or public relations) and has little or no involvement in any of the key areas affecting customer satisfaction, such as:

- ☐ *Product Policy.* Service levels, warranties, quality control, packaging, and labeling
- ☐ *New Product Development.* Specific customer needs and concerns, deficiencies of existing products, concept development
- ☐ *Communications.* Advertising messages and promises, sales attitudes, intermediary standards
- ☐ *Pricing.* Customer credit, price levels, and positioning

A mid-1970s study of 125 large national firms produced strong evidence of the isolation of the complaints and consumer affairs departments. More than 40 percent of the respondents indicated that their department was involved in fewer than two functions among those listed previously. On the average, complaint departments were involved in fewer than one-third of the 14 basic areas of marketing decisions examined. Only in one firm was consumer affairs involved in all aspects of product development, marketing, and sales.

When the researchers analyzed the relationship between the level of complaints received by the firm and complaint department input into marketing, they found a negative relationship: "The greater the . . . complaints the less the involvement of the complaint department in marketing decisions." Put another way, firms with the greatest need for information from complaints or consumer affairs departments appeared to pay the least attention to those departments. This was especially apparent in key areas such as product policy, new product development, communications, promotion, and pricing. In these areas there was a negative correlation between the level of complaints received and complaint department participation.

The defensive, reactive approach to customer complaints, coupled with the low visibility given to the customer affairs function, ensures that there will be no strategy for dealing with customers' complaints and needs. Consequently, these firms are preoccupied with complaint handling—responding to the immediate, day-to-day pressures created by specific problems. Lacking the systems and, perhaps even more important, the corporate vision to separate the key "signals" from the "noise" of customer complaints, they cannot make the necessary changes in product design, sales attitudes, advertising, pricing, and so on. Even in the face of overwhelming evidence, such firms ignore or refuse to accept that customers are dissatisfied for valid reasons related to the firm's actions.

☐ As early as 1970, Detroit automakers had clear indications that imported cars, particularly Japanese and West German models, were substantially superior to domestic cars in reliability, in "fits and finishes," and in overall customer value. Yet it has taken the Big Three almost 15 years even to begin to respond to the challenge.

☐ For years, Eastern Airlines has had a poor reputation for customer service, ranking high in the CAB's report on customer complaints per thousand passengers. Despite many public promises and changes in management, Eastern's performance in this area did not improve, nor did its financial situation.

## CUSTOMERS WANT FAIR TREATMENT

By and large, customers want to be treated fairly; their expectations are not unrealistic. Farmers, for example, know that they work their tractors, combines, and other equipment very hard. They are aware, therefore, that the equipment will fail occasionally and, within those limits, don't complain about failure frequency. Most buyers of household appliances know that, occasionally, one of their purchases will require service. In general:

☐ Only a small minority (10 to 15 percent) expect the "ideal" response from a company to a complaint;

☐ The majority of customers fall into two categories—*expected* or "what will be" and *deserved* or "what should be";

☐ A significant proportion of customers (20 to 30 percent) don't know how the company will respond.

Although some customers may complain because they believe they can get something out of complaining (a coupon, a refund, complimentary drinks), the vast majority take a more reasonable attitude; they want attention and some genuine effort at satisfaction.

## COMPLAINT HANDLING AFFECTS REPEAT PURCHASES AND LOYALTY

How a company meets the needs of customers when they are dissatisfied has a significant effect on customer loyalty.

☐ Poor complaint handling reduces customer loyalty, often dramatically.

☐ Effective responses to customer complaints increase satisfaction and brand loyalty.

☐ Customers who complain are often repeat purchasers and powerful influencers.

☐ Customers want genuine attention, not a token or form-letter response.

A survey of 2300 car owners who had at least one warranty repair performed on their car showed that (1) at least one-fourth were dissatisfied with warranty service, with repeat visits cited as the major cause of dissatisfaction; (2) about one-half of those who were dissatisfied said they would not buy another car from the same manufacturer; and (3) 25 percent of those who wouldn't repurchase had bought their last two cars from the same manufacturer.

At a hotel in the northeastern United States, a survey of guests who had written to management regarding problems showed:

Fifty percent would return to the hotel, while 30 percent would not;

How the complaint was handled drastically influenced whether they would advise their friends to stay at the hotel;

The substance of the complaint and the way it was handled had a great deal to do with a guest's decision to return to or stay away from the hotel; and

Nearly 30 percent of those who complained would have been satisfied with a proper response from management, better communications, or a more pleasant relationship.

Jaguar provides perhaps the most dramatic example of how company responses to customer complaints affect satisfaction and loyalty. In the 1960s and 1970s, Jaguar (then part of British Leyland) had a reputation for producing beautiful but unreliable cars. The saying was, "If you're going to buy a Jaguar, buy two—one to drive and the other for parts." By the mid-1980s, Jaguar had risen in rank to be next to Mercedes-Benz as a leader among luxury car producers in overall customer satisfaction, according to at least one survey; also, for the first time in years, customers had high repeat purchase intentions. "We are now selling to normal, mainstream people rather than enthusiasts," Jaguar's John Egan said.

Jaguar accomplished this feat through four key steps:

☐ *It Acknowledged the Problem.* The company made it crystal clear to its dealers and customers that (1) it knew they were concerned, even upset; (2) it realized that they had reasons to be upset; and (3) it knew the company had to take the lead in making the changes.

☐ *It Made Necessary Changes.* Jaguar changed its design and manufacturing procedures, weeded out suppliers who were of poor or unreliable quality, invested in new tooling and automation, and so on.

☐ *It Communicated Its Commitment.* The firm used a number of devices to tell its customers of the changes: longer, no-questions-asked warranties; performance comparisons; and individual attention to key corporate customers.

☐ *It Backed Up Words with Actions.* Management made certain its actions met its stated goals. Jaguar bent over backward to resolve customer complaints favorably, terminated recalcitrant dealers and those with inadequate service facilities, set up extensive testing facilities, increased parts warehousing and distribution, and so forth.

### Facts, Not Fluff

Note that there were few, if any, symbolic gestures or media events—no large advertisements signaling change, no photographs of company executives wielding wrenches, no public *mea culpas*. Instead Jaguar paid attention to basics: It improved its listening, it made necessary (even painful) changes, it ensured that the changes stuck, and it communicated with its customers.

# MOVE FROM COMPLAINT HANDLING TO CUSTOMER COMMUNICATIONS

A hotel guest found a fly in his soup and wrote an irate letter of complaint to the management expressing his feelings at some length. He immediately received a lengthy letter from the manager expressing regret at the whole incident and assuring him that the manager had *personally* reviewed the kitchen's cleanliness and had rebuked the chef and his assistants most severely. Unfortunately, someone had carelessly enclosed the original letter of complaint along with the manager's reply on which the manager had scrawled, "Send him the fly-in-the-soup letter"!

This anecdote illustrates graphically almost everything that's wrong with how companies traditionally approach customer complaints. First, it was an obvious form letter. Second, it was also obviously insincere. Finally, it was patronizing if not downright insulting to the customer's intelligence.

### The Forward Pass

Football coaches have a saying, "When a quarterback throws a forward pass, three things can happen and two of them are bad." When customers are unhappy, whether because the product doesn't work, because they, as consumers, were oversold, or because the service was poor, five things can happen and four of them are bad:

☐ *The Customer Suffers in Silence.* Not good. The next time the customer purchases the product or service, he or she will have a negative attitude from the start.

☐ *The Customer Switches in Silence.* Not good, either. At most, the firm knows only that the customer switched, not why or how it can get him or her back.

☐ *The Customer Tells Friends and Neighbors.* Worse. The firm stands to lose several customers: the one originally dissatisfied plus all the people he or she influences.

☐ *The Customer Talks to Third Parties.* Worst of all. It can lead to lawsuits or investigations.

☐ *The Unhappy Customer Talks to the Company.* The only positive outcome. It gives the firm a second chance to understand the customer's needs, identify and correct the problems, and convert a dissatisfied customer into a happy buyer, one that will keep coming back.

### Company Choices

Firms can listen to customer complaints that happen to come in, or they can actively reach out and solicit customer comments. Firms can treat the symptoms, or they can attack the underlying causes.

Thus companies can choose from among four possible strategies in dealing with customer dissatisfaction: deflect complaints, give lip service, react to needs, or build bridges (see Figure 9.1).

☐ *Deflect Complaints.* This is the classic response: provide an explanation, an apology, a discount coupon, or even a refund. The general intent is to get the encounter over with as quickly as possible, without spending too much money. Although such an approach places minimal demands on the firm, it provides few, mostly short-term, benefits. It also creates the appearance that only the squeaky wheel gets the grease; in the long run, this alienates customers and tends to turn even minor problems into major confrontations.

☐ *Give Lip Service.* Some firms actively proclaim their desire for customer feedback through widely displayed customer comment cards, mailers, advertising messages, and employee questions and responses. However, all of this is

Company responses

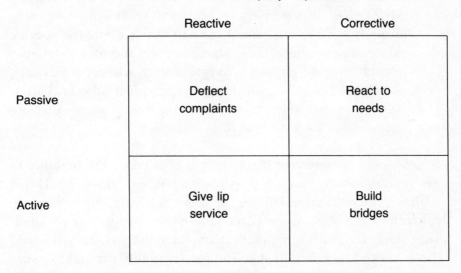

Figure 9.1 Strategies for dealing with complaints

merely superficial; although the company solicits customer input, it only treats the symptoms. The basic problems never seem to go away. In short, the firm is saying to the customer, "We're glad we were able to help you feel better. Now that you've got whatever it was off your chest, let's get back to where we were."

☐ *React to Needs.* Some firms are relatively passive listeners, but are quick to attack the specific causes of problems once the customer has made a complaint. This is often symptomatic of an engineering or technological bias within the firm. In other cases, companies have this reactive attitude because complaints come by way of a few strong customers, such as key distributors, which eliminates the need for the manufacturer to take an active role in soliciting complaints.

☐ *Build Bridges.* A few firms both encourage communication and treat underlying problems. Rather than wait for dissatisfied customers to get in touch with them, they actively seek out such customers and find out what is making them unhappy. They're also not content with solving the specific complaint; rather, they continuously monitor customer complaints and problems to isolate and, wherever possible, attack the causes—poor design, inadequate sales and after-sales support, incomplete operating instructions—that are responsible for customer dissatisfaction.

A great deal of customer discontent is created by the inability to get results when there is a problem. As explained by David Berliner at Consumers Union, "If there is a large manufacturer, consumers really go to the place where they bought the product. They feel, I think with justification, that the person who sold them the product should take the responsibility for making sure that the product works correctly, and if it doesn't, to take the product back. . . . People do that and are shocked, disappointed, and dismayed to find that they're not getting the support that they should have gotten and that once they've paid for the product, that's it—it 's over and done with and they're on their own."

Service industries, such as car rental agencies, banks, and restaurants, appear to follow a lip service strategy. They actively seek customer input by way of comment cards, evaluation forms, and employee training. However, their concern rarely appears to be more than skin-deep, as illustrated by the car rental firms' approach to a major customer irritant—the collision damage waiver. Many customers have complained repeatedly that this "option" is misleading, confusing, and extremely expensive in relation to the perceived benefits. There have been several investigations by various agencies. How have the firms responded? According to Shirley Goldinger, director of the Los Angeles County Department of Consumer Affairs, "There are so many flagrant abuses . . . it seems the industry is getting worse instead of better" (*WSJ*, April 14, 1987, p. 31).

The deflect complaints and give lip service strategies are characteristic of an approach that may be best described as *complaint handling*. This is characterized by a focus on the technical and tactical aspects of customer complaints and problems, such as:

☐ Responding rapidly to all customer communications,

☐ Disposing of complaints quickly and fairly,

☐ Keeping the cost of processing complaints to a minimum.

Customer satisfaction under this approach is measured in terms of the ratio of complaints to sales, and reductions in complaint volume are taken to mean that customer satisfaction is increasing.

By contrast, *customer communication* is a much broader approach to managing customer dissatisfaction. Its objectives are:

☐ To ensure that unvoiced dissatisfaction is as low as possible,

☐ To satisfy customers on an individual basis by providing assistance, refunds, and guidance as appropriate

☐ To determine the causes of recurring complaints and to recognize customer needs that the firm's products and services are not addressing

Building bridges is the ultimate example of this approach. However, the react to needs strategy is often an intermediate step in the transition from complaint handling to customer communications. Apple Computer, for example, has been quick to fix problems with its microcomputers but, in the past, has been slow in reaching out to customers to determine their problems. Whirlpool was one of the first to institute a toll-free number for customer problems—Cool-Line®—but was comparatively late in using customer surveys, focus groups, and other active methods of customer input.

Complaint handling is inherently limited in scope, because it deals primarily with the minority of customers who bother to complain to the firm. Customer communication, on the other hand, recognizes:

Customer complaints are an outward expression of customer dissatisfaction;

Most customer dissatisfaction occurs because customers' expectations have not been met; and

It is in the firm's long-term interest that dissatisfied customers be encouraged to communicate with the company, as opposed to suffering in silence, switching, or telling others of their complaints.

Consequently, where complaint handling often focuses on reducing the number of complaints, a customer communications strategy requires that the company *maximize* complaints.

### Making It Happen

Implementing a customer communication-oriented approach to customer problems requires major changes in corporate attitudes and focus, in managerial incentives and measurements, in the systems used to receive and monitor customer inputs, in the influence of the complaints function, and in the manner in which customer feedback is incorporated into the activities of the line functions. In each of these areas, a customer communication strategy differs significantly from more traditional approaches (Table 9.4). In our research, we found the following key characteristics distinguished companies that used a customer communications strategy:

**TABLE 9.4   Complaint Handling versus Customer Communication:
Key Differences**

|  | Complaint Handling | Customer Communication |
|---|---|---|
| Attitude | "Handle" the problem— make the complainer go away | Find out where the problem is and fix it |
| Focus | Complaint minimization | Build and increase customer loyalty |
| Incentives | Cost oriented | Long-term profit |
| Strategies | Varied—appeasement to indifference | Solution oriented, activist |
| Customer communication | Minimal; primarily customer initiated— cards, letters, telephones | Systematic; mix of customer and company-initiated communication |
| Standards | Focus on satisfying— meeting demands/need of *average* customer | Emphasis on excelling— meeting expectations of the most demanding customer |
| Systems | Few/no organized approaches to collecting, monitoring and analyzing customer problems | A coordinated system for customer communications and fees to affected department |
| Location |  | Staff function |
| Input/ influence | Minimal or nonexistent | Significant influence all key areas |
| Changes in response to complaint | Minimal or reactive | Anticipate/rapid response to changing customer needs |

☐ *Top-Down Commitment.* L.L. Bean's approach to customer problems is perhaps the most vivid example of the fundamental differences in corporate attitudes toward customer complaints. At L.L. Bean, as all of its regular customers know, the return policy is very simple: Goods can be returned at any time. Almost from the inception of the firm, L.L. Bean has refunded the customer's money with "no reasons necessary, no excuse required, no abuse of the article too strong to justify refusing a refund." In short, it is a 100 percent guarantee. Essentially, the company is saying to its customers, "If you're dissatisfied with the product at any time, bring it back, no matter when you purchased it or how long you've used it." Although other firms, notably Sears, have similar guarantees, L.L. Bean's policy is unique, and symptomatic of the company's approach to customer problems: No sale is final until the customer is completely satisfied.

☐ *Innovative Strategies.* Some companies, recognizing that customers are often unsure about how to complain, have taken innovative approaches: An English shoe store chain provides it customers with a handy guide detailing how (and to whom) they should complain if they have a problem with their purchase. Proctor & Gamble places a toll-free 800 number on every one of its products, enabling customers to contact the firm rapidly in case of problems.

☐ *Extensive Investment in Customer Feedback Systems.* Nearly all of these firms have made substantial investments in building and maintaining customer communication and feedback systems. Every month, for example, Xerox surveys 10 percent of the population owning each of their machines (48,000 customer surveys). All problems are referred to the appropriate sales or service branches for follow-up and resolution. In addition, Xerox service personnel are encouraged to make follow-up telephone calls after each service visit to find out if the problem has been fixed and if there are any other problems, and to obtain additional customer feedback.

☐ *Managerial Incentives and Measurements that Emphasize the Importance of Customer Feedback.* Many of the companies we interviewed emphasize to their managers the importance of paying attention to what the customers are saying. Managers are encouraged to talk to customers and listen to their complaints. Xerox, for example, bases part of its engineers' performance evaluations, and therefore their compensation, on customer satisfaction.

# 10

## Corporate Values

### THE SOFTWARE

Corporate values are the drivers behind all decisions regarding product, sales, and after sales. In companies where the basic corporate values are customer focused, the other three elements almost always act in harmony, thereby ensuring that customers will be happy with the firm and its products. By contrast, whenever customer satisfaction is excluded from the firm's basic beliefs and tenets, the other three components cannot produce the desired impact. Corporate values, in other words, are the software which decide whether the firm will allocate resources—financial, technical, and human—to maximizing customer satisfaction.

The reasons are obvious: First, corporate values define the culture of the company. Second, corporate values drive behavior at all levels, but especially at the operational, day-to-day level which can make or break customer satisfaction in the long run. Third, corporate values reinforce the incentives and measurements which the firm uses in implementing its strategies.

The firms we researched fully understand the importance of corporate values in their efforts to keep customers happy. While the specific approach varied with the individual firm, we identified the following common characteristics:

- [ ] They made customer satisfaction central to the firm's beliefs and values.
- [ ] They used formal symbols and systems to communicate the importance of customer satisfaction within the firm.
- [ ] They used informal symbols and systems to ensure that the firm achieved its goal of keeping customers happy.

## WHY NECESSARY

Explicitly customer-oriented corporate values are essential for three reasons: First, they help the firm—and particularly its managers—maintain its focus on the customer, despite any temporary distractions. Second, they help defuse the quantitative versus qualitative conflicts discussed earlier, that is, the fact that most cost savings can be quantified while the benefits of many investments in improving customer satisfaction are often intangible or difficult to measure. Finally, explicit customer-oriented corporate values ensure that the firm will continue to make the necessary long-term investments in customer satisfaction.

Harvey Lamm, president of Subaru of America, puts it thus, "When a company first starts, the biggest concern for everyone is 'How do you make the first sale?' [A]s the firm starts to build a market position, then the focus of the executive moves more toward management and a lot of different areas . . . that take him away from the concerns of the marketplace. When his sales and marketing people tell him of their needs, he is not very receptive and he is more focused on how he can manage the company and build profitability. And when they ask for financial support in dealing with satisfying the customer, either through the development of the product or the after-service for the product, he is not inclined to support that kind of request. He sort of sees that as *their* problem and as soon as that message gets through the organization, I think that's when the firm starts taking the customer for granted."

He goes on to add that, "The way you prevent it from occurring is *caring*. They [the top managers] have to have a caring attitude and a clear understanding that *that's* really their future, that profits are really dependent on customer satisfaction. . . . It all starts with the fiber of the business and the fiber of the company. Nobody in our company would need to do something like that [try to quantify the effects of a particular investment in customer satisfaction] . . . because everybody is focused on the understanding that the product and service have to meet customers' needs. To satisfy the customer everybody in the company has to understand that the total existence of the company depends on the customer, so if the customer is not satisfied, he is not going to be a customer tomorrow [and] we don't have a business tomorrow. So unless people understand that, and understand that each of them makes a contribution toward satisfying the customer, whether it be direct or indirect, then I don't think that you get anything happening. I don't think those decisions [about investing in customer satisfaction] ever come up in a company that doesn't have that kind of a [customer-focused] philosophy."

## VALUES DEFINE CULTURE

Culture is often defined as a society's (or company's) "design for living." Corporate values are then the firm's *reasons for living*. They define what the firm and its employees want out of commercial life—growth, financial performance, profitability, industry leadership, technological leadership, customer loyalty—and in what order of priority. By setting this "cultural agenda," corporate values tell everyone—employees, managers, stockholders, suppliers, competitors, and customers—what the company believes is *really* important to the firm, that is, how the firm will react when push comes to shove. Corporate values also determine the framework within which key issues are decided and resources allocated.

Not surprisingly, the customer—and customer satisfaction—was a key part of the corporate values of all firms we interviewed (our winners). At Federal Express, for example, according to Robert Hernandez, vice president of customer service, the firm's values are, "People, service, profits. It's the corporate philosophy that the company grew up with and is embedded deeply in every employee who works at Federal Express. I believe it's in that order—people, service, profits—for a reason. [It] tells you automatically that service is there, but it also gives you a clue as to what takes the lead in this corporation . . . and that is the basic people operation. Beyond that, we know we're a service business. We know that what we ship is so critical there are not a lot of second chances. So you have to do it right the first time, you have to do what you say, and if you do that and do that consistently, people are going to come back to Federal Express."

Jim Blue of Boeing describes the situation as follows, "There has always been from a cultural standpoint a very strong relationship to our customers. Partially because it started so few in numbers and the relationships were so personal. The 707 was launched with a handshake between Juan Trippe [of Pan Am] and T. Wilson, president of Boeing. Not with a lot of paper and detail, but 'I'll build you an airplane that will do the job.' . . . The attitude is one of, 'That's something we promised, that's much more of a commitment.' That word [commitment] carries tremendous clout in this company. If you commit to do something, you *will* perform."

According to one executive at Xerox, the focus is on "profit, employee and customer. [I] like to think that customer is the base of that triangle, not just because it's the longest word, but because without your customer base you have neither one of these." Among Northwestern Mutual's guiding principles, first written in an executive committee decree of 1888, is that "Northwestern will not seek to be the biggest, but the best. It will put policyowners first and will attempt to provide fair and equal treatment to all policyowners, those who bought insurance many years ago as well as those buying it today." At Swissair the focus is on "providing customers in the air and on the ground outstanding service in keeping with the traditions of Swiss hospitality."

These and similar sentiments at the other firms we researched were not merely lip service; rather, they were expressed by people at every level within and outside the company. In short, they were truly the values of the firm, rooted deeply in everyone's consciousness.

Inevitably, these values create a cultural pressure to be customer-oriented, to want to do everything possible to keep the customer happy. Newcomers to the organization who may or may not share this customer focus either adapt or soon feel uncomfortable, out-of-place, and leave. As several participants put it, "Sometimes you run into an executive who doesn't want that pressure [to be customer focused]. It's impossible for him to survive in our organization."

In addition, these values produce an important, if intangible, pro-customer bias within the organization. This bias effectively preempts any protracted discussions of trade-offs between customer satisfaction and cost. One fact that came out very strongly in all our interviews was that these firms did not view the issue of customer satisfaction as negotiable, "so much customer satisfaction for so much cost savings or whatever." They simply don't think of it that way. As Gerd Klauss of Mercedes-Benz put it, "In engineering there's no question of doing trade-off analyses [between cost and customer satisfaction]. We're obsessed with this." Kerney Laday of Xerox expressed the same sentiments: "What happens in either of those systems [cost-focused vs. customer-focused] is that this internal struggle always goes on between the two dichotomies; that's not how to look for the answer." This attitude can only be understood in the context of the strong corporate values that create a cultural emphasis on maximizing customer satisfaction.

## VALUES DRIVE BEHAVIOR

Customer-oriented values inevitably lead to behavior that's focused on maximizing customer satisfaction. This becomes apparent in how people at all levels and in every function think about the nature of their business and respond to customer needs, what they expect of themselves, their co-workers, managers, and intermediaries, occasionally even in the types of promotions and contests they engage in:

☐ As Bruce Oseland of Century 21 Real Estate Corporation states, "We don't have a product. The product we sell in our advertising is someone who wears a gold coat and the image and service capabilities of that individual. . . . It's simply, 'Here's what you can expect when you walk into a Century 21® office and do business with a Century 21®-affiliated salesperson.' . . . [But as a result] the real estate salespeople and the real estate brokers [have] started thinking more about, 'If I serve my client's needs in the manner in which I have been trained to do, the money will come,' as opposed to, 'If I sell that house, I get $4000 commission from it.' That is bad thinking and a whole lot of people starved thinking in that fashion and didn't know why they starved."

☐ Boeing's Phil Condit says, "I get calls that are related to when I was chief engineer on the 757. 'We got a problem.' The answer isn't 'Hey, look, that's not my job anymore, I am now head of sales.' We don't have anybody around that would give you that kind of answer, we really don't. They've just fallen by the wayside. The response is 'Let *me* [emphasis added] get back to you. I'll go work at it.' Or if it's very identifiable to a person, we'll say, 'The person that can handle that problem for you is this person. Here's his phone number.' . . . Again, that doesn't always work, and every once in a while we get a customer that comes in and says, 'We used to feel like we always got a response and we don't have that feeling now.' So we all go stare at each other and say, 'Why is that? Why is that customer making statements like that?' Sometimes it will be because they had a salesman who performed exactly as Dean [Dean Thornton, president of Boeing Commercial Aircraft] stated. He was their surrogate, and fought valiantly, and that has changed for whatever reason. We need that advocate in the system again."

☐ According to a Maytag executive: "We started manufacturing automatic washers in 1949. [It was really 1950 before it got into full production.] To celebrate the 25th anniversary of our manufacturing automatic washers, we held a contest. . . . We offered a prize of something like $5000 for the oldest operating Maytag [automatic] washer. [We] felt that we would have something like 2000 or 3000 entries and that would be that. We ended up with 30,000+ entries and the washer that we ended up awarding the prize to was something like the 13th one we manufactured. . . . Now that's a testament to the kind of quality we built into the washer from the very beginning. But it is also a testament to . . . the availability of parts and [the] serviceability of it, because the one that won the prize was in its third life, I think. It had been bought, used by the original purchaser, turned in or sold to somebody . . . and when we finally caught up with it in this contest, they had bought it for (I think) $50. They got $5000 for it. But in the third life, somebody had to do a little bit of repair, I'm sure. And the availability of parts then becomes very significant."

Century 21's® focus on customer needs, Boeing's insistence that whoever receives a call from a customer be responsible for following up on it, Maytag's interest in finding out what happened to its first automatic washers—they all reveal these firms' concern for customer satisfaction in action.

## VALUES OVERLAY INCENTIVES AND MEASUREMENTS

The values of the firm also have a strong influence on how it evaluates and rewards its employees. In companies where customer satisfaction is a key concern, there is great emphasis on rewarding people who provide superior customer service or satisfaction. Nor are these rewards always lavish; to the contrary, our research indicated that, for the most part, they are more symbolic than monetary—a little sticker, a pin proclaiming the importance of the customer, or a pat on the back. Much more important were the recognition and the reaffirmation of the corporate values and culture that these symbols provided.

Conversely, the incentives and measurements used by a firm are the litmus test of its values, a very visible way for all—employees, managers, dealers, suppliers, and customers—to determine whether the company really means what it says, that is, what are the *real* values of the firm. In many cases the two are inconsistent; the overt—or publicly articulated—values are customer-focused, while the real values, as revealed through the rewards and punishments, are the other way. Detroit traditionally has blamed most of its customer problems on the dealers, but its internal measurements and rewards have always stressed units sold, not customer satisfaction—despite all the advertising about "Mr. Goodwrench" and "The customer is job one." Therefore it's not surprising that dealers, in turn, pay little attention to customer satisfaction, as demonstrated by the low level of "Same dealer purchase intent" indicated in various surveys. (See Chapter 1.)

Further, the wrong incentives can actually detract from customer satisfaction. Bernhard Oettli of Swissair points out that "we've never had an incentive pay system (to make the cabin crew be more customer-oriented). American Airlines once had a system where they tried to measure the people-to-people performance of their crew by a very elaborate system where observers were sitting in the cabin and noting how many positive contacts they were making and finishing, and so on. It didn't work. It goes with the perversion of all kinds of such mechanical systems: [because] you can't order people to be friendly with passengers, you then take out one element that means that. You can observe that somebody goes to another person, talks to him and smiles. . . . When you introduce such a system, you might have quite a positive effect at the beginning, but people are no fools. They understand what you're up to, and they play the system then, instead of playing the quality you want."

## MAKING IT HAPPEN

Nearly every firm pays lip service to the importance of customer satisfaction through mission statements ("we seek to increase customer value"), slogans ("the customer is king"), motivational devices ("fan appreciation nights") and all the other paraphernalia. But the real attitude is "can't fail"—almost as though the firm is saying, "Regardless of how we treat them, customers will continue to buy our products." Consequently, the question we kept asking ourselves was, What's the secret? What are these companies doing that's different? Why did customer-focused corporate values take hold in *these* firms and not at others in their industries?

In our interviews we probed hard to determime *how* these companies managed to make their corporate values come alive. However, the harder we pushed, the less satisfying were the answers
we received. It was as if the interviewees either didn't know how
they could explain it any differently, or else felt that it was so obvious as to need no further clarification. As one of the managers
at Maytag put it, "Over the years, many times I've had people ask
me, 'What is the secret of Maytag?' There is no secret you can
identify. It's many things, but at the heart of it is this dedication to
quality throughout the company." Repeatedly, in company after
company, interviewees at all levels expressed their sentiments
similarly. They felt—nay, were convinced—that their firm's success was tied to a companywide dedication to quality, customer
satisfaction, service, or performance.

Nor was the answer to be found in external attributes such as corporate style or measurement and monitoring systems. We wish
we could say that these firms' key to success was to have a "pas-
sion for keeping the customer happy" or that they "made their
strategy happen" by using elaborate measurements and incentives. Unfortunately, our winners don't fall into any such convenient molds. On the contrary, we found that their styles varied all
the way from the evangelical approach used by Federal Express,
to the analytical style of Xerox or Swissair. Nor did it follow that
evangelical firms operated intuitively while analytical ones used
lots of measurements. (See Figure 10.1.) Several firms who were
quite passionate about their commitment to customer satisfaction
nevertheless used measurements extensively. By contrast, others
more analytical in style had no elaborate systems; they operated
on a much more intuitive basis than the passionate firms; Delta
Airlines apparently doesn't even carry out surveys of customer
satisfaction.

### Visible and Invisible Systems

We believe that the key to these firms' success in translating their
corporate values lies in their ability to reinforce the messages car-

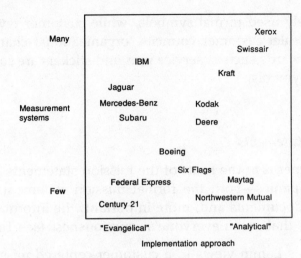

*Figure 10.1 How our winners' styles varied*

ried by *visible symbols* such as corporate mission statements, customer satisfaction measurements, and formal incentives with *invisible systems*—the training their people receive, whom they promote and why, how they make and reinforce key decisions, and the degree to which their senior management gets involved in understanding customers' needs and concerns. This has two benefits: First, everybody gets a clear, consistent message that keeping the customer happy is essential to the firm's (and their) success. Second, there's no wasted motion—in finding out what management *really* wants, in responding to periodic crash programs to improve customer satisfaction, in paying lip service, and so forth.

## VISIBLE SYMBOLS

The companies we interviewed use a number of devices, both formal and informal, to convey the importance of customer satisfaction to their employees, managers, suppliers, and customers. Mission statements and incentives/measurements are two of the most widely used formal symbols, while customer review committees, dealer/customer councils, organizational changes, and informal awards such as service pins and stickers are some of the informal symbols.

### Mission Statements

The customer is at the heart of the mission statements at each of these companies—both the formal mission statements used in company documents and, more important, the informal mission statements that are in everyone's consciousness (see Table 10.1).

As Subaru's Lamm views it, a customer-centered mission statement is an essential prerequisite for creating the right philosophy. "It [a customer-oriented philosophy] depends on what comes down from the top. It doesn't come from the bottom up. It has to come from the top down. Because unless the attitude is developed from the top down, you are not going to get the motivation, the direction of the people. . . . You are either a customer-focused company or you are not. And I don't think that you can go after the problem with mandates. I think you have to have a total direction. It has to be a fiber, the mission of the company . . . that all of

**TABLE 10.1  Some Informal Mission Statements**

| Company | |
| --- | --- |
| Boeing | Keeping commitments |
| Deere | Keep the customer running |
| Jaguar | Rebuilding quality image |
| Kodak | You push the button, we do the rest |
| Northwestern Mutual Life Insurance | Not the biggest, but best |
| Federal Express | People, service, profits |
| Maytag | Quality |
| Subaru | Customer satisfaction |
| Mercedes-Benz | The best or nothing |
| Xerox | Profit, employee and customer |
| Swissair | Swiss hospitality |

the people of the company have to understand what [it] is all about. [And] unless customer satisfaction is a very, very key focus in the mission statement, it's not going to work."

### Incentives and Measurements

Behind the mission statement, of course, you have to have policies and procedures that are supportive of the mission. In the words of Xerox's Laday, "We have that [customer satisfaction] as a statement and we have processes as result of that statement . . . We're creating a system and are teaching and putting in place processes, words, language, tools to understand in a more rational way [the] customer and how you go about getting that quality to the customer. We have some processes that teach us just who is the customer, what are the customer's requirements, how do we meet those requirements. We're not just teaching in a way that says, 'Customer is king,' we're teaching [it] in the way of requirements . . . [by which] we mean what's necessary, what's right on the mark to get their business and do it for them."

Of particular importance are the systems used to measure customer satisfaction and the incentives provided to employees, managers, and even to customers, to ensure that the firm's objective of keeping the customer happy is met. As the quote from Laday suggests, Xerox carries out extensive measurements of customer satisfaction *and* ties employee (and especially management) compensation explicitly to these measurements. For example, the chief engineer for any volume group of products such as the 1075 line of copiers has 25 percent of his performance evaluation based on the in-field performance of the machines, as measured by Xerox's own customer satisfaction management system. For field service managers, one-third of their performance appraisal (and therefore bonuses, promotions, etc.) is based on customer satisfaction. These highly explicit incentives are backed up by Xerox's customer surveys. Responses are tracked by a very comprehensive system, which not only ensures follow-up on all problems, but also provides detailed reports on the performance of field service personnel, managers, offices, machine-specific trends, and so forth.

Few companies tie performance evaluation so explicitly to customer satisfaction as Xerox does. In part, of course, this reflects differences in corporate style and in the nature of their products or services. Swissair, for instance, tracks customer reactions very closely but, as described earlier, refuses to tie it explicitly to cabin crew evaluations for fear that it would be counterproductive. Nonetheless, there is an implicit connection that is understood by all. Federal Express measures various aspects of its service such as speed of response to telephone inquiries, the percentage of packages that arrive at their destination before 10:30A.M., and the number of packages that are delayed. It also provides incentives to customers—yes, customers!—to ensure that the company lives up to its commitments. For example, Federal Express has money-back guarantees for on-time delivery and a thirty-minute response to any inquiries about the status of a package. Maytag appears to carry out relatively few measurements of customer satisfaction, nor does it provide explicit incentives for improving performance in this area. Similarly, other firms vary considerably in their approaches to tracking customer satisfaction and how explicitly they tie it into specific incentives.

Despite these differences in their approach to measurements and incentives, we observed the following common characteristics:

☐ *Measurements Were Externally Focused.* These firms don't rely on what *they* think the customer is saying about them. Instead, they actively search to find out, formally or informally, how satisfied customers are with their products and services.

☐ *Emphasis Was on Output Variables.* Our winners weren't interested in how much effort was put in, but what the outcome was, for example, the response time to answer a telephone call or wait on a customer, how long customers waited, how satisfied customers were with various aspects of the product or service, and so on.

☐ *Measurements Don't Become a Political Football.* In no instance did we find any suggestion that customer satisfaction measurements were disputed as being biased, not relevant to their industry, an aberration—all the excuses one hears when managers *don't* want to hear the bad news about customer satisfaction. In large part, we believe, this is due to the fact that the internal culture doesn't encourage such defenses. An equally important reason is the care that goes into these measurements to remove perceived or actual bias.

☐ *Information Was Shared Widely.* The results of customer satisfaction measurements were shared across the board, including functions such as finance which conventionally would not receive such data. There are several advantages to such widespread readership: First, everyone knew how well other departments were performing in keeping customers happy; this removed any uncertainties or doubts. Second, it let different parts of the company compare their performance with their counterparts in other regions or departments. This increased peer pressure to improve performance. Finally, by sharing the data widely these companies created the awareness that customer satisfaction was everyone's business and also permitted different departments to work together to solve problems. This is particularly important because frequently the causes—and therefore the cures—of customer dissatisfaction are spread across functions and departments.

☐ *Rewards Were Clearly Linked.* In each of these companies people understood that there was a definite link between their ability to keep customers happy and their rewards. By and large this was implicitly understood; only Xerox, among all the firms we interviewed, had an explicit link between customer satisfaction and employee/managerial performance evaluation. But in all cases there was no room for doubt in anyone's mind that keeping customers happy paid off, and that making or keeping them unhappy was definitely hazardous to one's future with the firm.

## Other Symbols

In addition to the mission statement and incentives/measurement systems, several firms used various other devices to communicate their dedication to customer satisfaction:

□ *A Policyowner's Examining Committee.* At Northwestern Mutual Life Insurance Co., five policyowners with no other connection with the firm are appointed by the board each year to spend five days at company expense examining, questioning, challenging, looking at the books, records, and so on. This tradition is nearly 70 years old; Northwestern is the only life insurance company operating with such comprehensive involvement by the customer. Committee members are often surprised at the openness of company personnel in answering questions, showing documents, and so forth. A summary of the committee's report is published in the annual report.

□ *A Customer Satisfaction Representative.* Subaru was the first to appoint a full-time manager in charge of customer satisfaction who crosses all corporate lines—service, sales, parts, and so on. As David Wager, the present incumbent, puts it, "My mission is twofold: First, to take a look at everything this corporation is doing, from whatever department, to determine how [Subaru] can increase its effect in generating customer satisfaction. Second, I am to look at, develop and implement new programs, policies and procedures that will impact on customer satisfaction in a favorable way. I don't handle the short-term, day-to-day, customer relations kind of things."

☐ *Dealer/Customer Councils.* Several firms that market through a dealer network have dealer councils that meet, often at company expense, to discuss problems and air their concerns with company executives. For example: Boeing creates a working group composed of personnel from different airlines to provide a forum for listening to the airlines.

☐ *Token Awards.* At Six Flags, employees who provide exceptional customer service receive little pins from their managers, which are worn proudly by all recipients. At Federal Express, similarly, managers give little stickers—Bravo-Zulus—which signify superior performance in providing service or satisfaction or performance.

## INVISIBLE SYSTEMS

We found that visible symbols were reinforced by a number of devices which we call "the hidden systems." In particular, the manner in which employees are selected and trained, how and with what inherent bias key decisions are made and how much Contact top management maintains with customer needs—how companies behaved in these three areas, we found, had a considerable impact on the firm's ability to translate its customer orientation into practice.

### Selection, Training, and Tenure

If there's one factor that distinguishes our winners in their ability to translate corporate values into action, it is their stress on customer satisfaction when selecting new employees, while training them and in promoting them. Each of the firms we interviewed placed great emphasis on ensuring that their systems for selection, training, and promotion acted as "filters" which would screen out persons whose values are not as customer-oriented as the firm would like. The reasons for this focus on selection, training, and tenure are obvious and best expressed by Boeing's Jim Blue, "We have all kinds of computer systems to try to improve our responsiveness. We spend a lot of money on that. All these systems are great, but the personal touch is really what makes it work."

The process of customer focus, we found, begins from the point at which potential new employees are screened and selected. Listen to Swissair's Oettli as he describes how cabin personnel are chosen, "We try to do personality screening as much as we can, to find the personalities which will *fit into that company culture of putting the passenger first* [emphasis added], being patient, not being authoritarian, not being bossy. We see these people for one day, for about five to six hours. We have a screening of applications, and then we invite groups of eight candidates and do the screening here, in-house. Of course, you can hit it or you can't. We then have a [rather] long probation period where we try to find out more about these people. It is only after three months' flying that they get a definite contract." Other firms use other, perhaps less formal systems, but the common thread still is the fit with the company culture, in which putting the customer first is always a central tenet.

While picking employees with the right attitude is obviously an important first step, these firms don't stop there; they ensure that they train their new employees—as well as old ones—to put the customer first. Some of the training may be formal, but much of it is informal. "They become believers by association, when they see the old-timers actually believing it and doing it," says Kodak's Donald Weller.

Occasionally this training—to make employees customer focused—may be quite revolutionary. For example, prior to the formation of national real estate organizations such as Century 21 Real Estate Corp., the average broker's education was very technical—how to get your license, very basic sales training, and so on. As Bruce Oseland of Century 21 Real Estate Corp. recalls, "Real estate training back at that time . . . didn't really tell you how to serve a customer, how to understand the trauma of moving across the country—they're not just out there to buy a house, they're changing their life. So Century 21® started developing training programs to take a real estate salesperson away from selling physical property, to better understand[ing] the motivation, better understand[ing] the trauma that's inherent in any move. . . . So Century 21® addressed in the training programs how to understand the emotional side of a real estate transaction and then how to serve the client's needs."

Further, all these firms see this investment in training as essential to their future, something that cannot be compromised because of transient financial constraints or budget cutting. As Kodak's John Barnes, vice president of customer and marketing support, views it, "The commitment to training is not, again, the 'nice' thing to do, or the 'appropriate' thing to do, it is absolutely mandatory, critical to our continued success. We're now looking at the skill, knowledge, and performance requirements to make superior performers, to ensure that, one, we're hiring right people, then teaching the skills necessary to perform in the highest-quality, world-class arena."

Finally, their promotion and tenure policies—how they decide whom to keep around and whom to promote—again reinforce the importance of being customer driven. Over and over again, in company after company, the response was, "We don't have anybody around that's not customer-oriented—they've just fallen by the wayside, or learn't that's not how you get ahead in this company or gone elsewhere or whatever."

### Key Decisions

Another important "hidden" system is how key decisions are made and what aspects or values are emphasized in making these decisions. In the companies we analyzed, it was evident that

> There was no question in anyone's mind about the *right* priorities; the customer was always first,
>
> Management supported this customer focus in both word and deed, and
>
> This customer focus showed up in decisions both large and small.

In his book, *The IBM Way*, Buck Rodgers tells the story of being late for a meeting with the CEO, Tom Watson, Jr., because of a customer call that came up unexpectedly. What's interesting about this anecdote is what it reveals about IBM's focus on the customer. Rodgers *knew* what the right priorities were, namely the customer problem first, the meeting with Watson second. He felt confident enough about the values of the firm to make the decision to be late for the meeting, *without hesitation*. Watson, Jr. supported Rodger's decision without questioning, second guessing, or undue complaining.

Neel Hall, now senior vice president in charge of Deere's farm equipment division, made the same point while discussing a problem he faced earlier in his career: "When I went to Europe 17 years ago, . . . [o]ne of the first real problems that I encountered was the fact that we had a severe engine problem. I knew what our forecasted loss was; I knew what our sales were going to be because I was responsible for them at the time; I figured out what it was going to cost us to fix those engines, because it was all the engines that we had sold for, I don't know, four or five years. It was going to cost something around $5 million, on top of a more than $20 million loss, related to less than $200 million worth of sales. I knew that if we didn't do it, $200 million [in sales] would become a lot less than that. There are lot of things in the company that you can spend a whole lot of time on, but getting the decision to commit to making the product right was about as easy a decision as I was ever able to get, and it was within literally a matter of minutes. I'd spent a long, long time being sure I had the facts . . . and the identification of the problem was clear, (as was) the solution. But we immediately said, 'Well, we've got to do what's right. If we're going to stay in business over here, we've got to do it.' "

Over time, anecdotes such as these become part of the folklore of the company, reinforcing corporate values and providing guidance and reassurance to employees in making decisions that affect the customer. This creates an intangible feedback mechanism which helps frame issues in terms of their impact on the customer, thereby ensuring that the conditioned reflexes of managers and employees are geared toward keeping customers happy.

### Top Management Contact with Customers

The senior managers of the firms we interviewed took pains to stay *personally* close to their customers. Many of the executives made it a point to respond individually to customers who contacted them directly; a couple went further and personally monitored the subsequent corrective actions for a sampling of all complaint letters. Several executives also participated in frequent formal and informal meetings with their customers and listened to what they had to say regarding the company, its products and services, and their experiences, problems, and concerns. At some firms—for example, Boeing and Deere—senior executives maintained their contacts with key customers long after their direct sales or customer service responsibilities had ended. In addition, quite a few of the managers indicated that they acted as customers on their days off; that is, they unpinned their badges of rank, put on casual clothes, and purchased the products or services that their firms manufactured, just to get a "customer's eye-view" of the firm. Nor was this desire to "stay close to the customer" merely lip service; these executives devoted a significant part of their time—between 10 and 20 percent—to these activities.

Taken together, all of these activities create a third hidden system that has both symbolic and operational value. On the symbolic level the benefits are twofold. First, the rest of the firm realizes that top management is serious and committed to the proposition that "keeping customers happy is good business." Nothing drives home the point that the customer is important as much as the sight of the chief executive standing in line for a ticket (Six Flags), or a senior manager putting on a steward's jacket and staffing a flight (Swissair), or a vice president in charge of service handling a telephone call from a former customer in person (Boeing). On the other hand, nothing demoralizes the troops so much as a senior manager who is obviously unfamiliar, or worse yet, unconcerned about customers' needs and reactions.

At the same time, the outside world—suppliers, dealers, distributors, and, ultimately, customers—realizes that "this firm means business when it says the customer is number one." The benefits of this are subtle but highly significant. Suppliers and intermediaries realize that they too must conform to this ethic; this reduces wasted motion by discouraging others who are less customer-oriented from working with the firm, thereby diverting or dissipating its resources. It also acts as an external feedback system, as suppliers and intermediaries direct the firm's attention to problems it might otherwise have overlooked.

In addition, this system had considerable operational value. By the very nature of their jobs, senior managers tend to become increasingly isolated from customers by other concerns—production problems, governmental regulations, shareholder demands, personnel issues, and so forth. This isolation is made worse by the very human reluctance to be the bearer of bad news; their subordinates tend to tone down or even hide customer complaints and grievances. To break out of this protective cocoon it is necessary for the manager to force himself or herself to deal with customers "on-line," where the immediacy of the complaints and the intensity of the reactions strips away all the protective layers and forces the manager to confront unpleasant realities. For this to occur, there is no alternative but to deal directly with customers by reviewing actual complaints, riding around with account executives, cultivating and maintaining close relations with typical customers, and so on. Memos, reports, survey statistics, and other indirect methods just don't have the same immediacy or impact. What's more, they fail to develop that intuitive judgment that's so necessary to prevent false starts, that sixth sense that tells executives whether a proposed pricing scheme, product change or warranty program is "fair" to the customer.

# Index

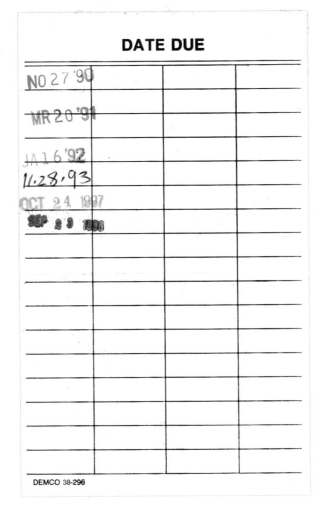

**DATE DUE**

| | | |
|---|---|---|
| NO 27 '90 | | |
| MR 20 '91 | | |
| JA 16 '92 | | |
| 11.28.93 | | |
| OCT 24 1997 | | |
| SEP 23 1998 | | |
| | | |
| | | |
| | | |
| | | |
| | | |
| | | |
| | | |
| | | |

DEMCO 38-296